Evangelism and Theology
in the
Wesleyan Spirit

BY ALBERT C. OUTLER

DISCIPLESHIP RESOURCES

MATERIALS FOR GROWTH IN CHRISTIAN FAITH & LIFE

Nashville, Tennessee

P.O. Box 840 • Nashville, TN 37202 • Phone (615) 340-7068

Library of Congress Catalog Card No. 95-83588

ISBN 0-88177-151-1

DR151

Introduction

Ezra Earl Jones

James Russell Lowell's words:

> *New occasions teach new duties, time makes ancient good uncouth;*
> *They must upward still and onward, who would keep abreast of truth.*

present the perennial problem and continuing challenge confronting the Christian believer today. We, who are standing on the threshold of a new millennium, have the vantage point of seeing the "old" that must pass away and at the same time helping create the "new" that must yet be.

Today, I believe the "new" is centered in a spiritual quest. It seems that the whole world is on a spiritual quest. Signs of spiritual renaissance are to be found everywhere. Other signs, however, indicate that many present-day major denominations continue on "activity quests" rather than "spiritual quests."

John R. Mott saw this trend more than fifty years ago. His words were: "An alarming weakness among Christians is that we are producing Christian activities faster than we are producing Christian experience and Christian faith. The disciplining of our souls and the deepening of our acquaintance with God are not proving sufficiently thorough to enable us to meet the unprecedented expansion of opportunity and responsibility of our generation."

The General Board of Discipleship believes that what needs to be working in the church are settings where people can seek God. Our task is to help the church create arenas for seeking God, practicing the spiritual disciplines and working on faith development.

Because of our commitment to this "spiritual quest" we are continuing to make available some of the basic resources which serve as foundation pieces for people sharing this quest. This book, *Evangelism and Theology in the Wesleyan Spirit*, by Albert C. Outler, focuses on gaining knowledge of the God and the Christ whom we serve and using that knowledge to become the spiritual leaders and present-day disciples which we must become as we make Him known.

Dr. Outler's life spanned the twentieth century. Few other United Methodists have been called upon to serve their church in as many important roles as he has. A distinguished scholar, he served in professional capacities at Yale, Duke and Southern Methodist Universities and gave the Dudleian Lectures at Harvard University. He served as chairman of the Theological Study Commission on Doctrine and Doctrinal Standards of his church, and was a distinguished member of the Academic Council Jerusalem Institute for Advanced Theological Studies in Jerusalem. He was a member of the World Council of Churches, and the World Methodist Council-Secretariat for Promoting Christian Unity, among many other organizations.

Evangelism in the Wesleyan Spirit was first presented as the Denman Lectures in New Orleans, Louisiana in January 1971. These lectures were established to honor the life and ministry of Dr. Harry Denman, retired General Secretary of the General Board of Evangelism of the former Methodist Church.

The "activism" of the 1960's and 1970's brought about a resurgence of Outler's strong desire to deal with the essential, radical questions for a new generation. These were questions like: What is the nature of the gospel? What is the good news? Is Jesus Christ really Lord? Are the claims of the Christian faith of having a unique position among the religions of the world really valid? In addressing these issues you step into the inner sanctum of Outler's soul's struggle to provide answers for today's Christian.

The unique contribution which he has made to this ongoing evangelism dialogue is at the point of the application of the Wesleyan ministry, coupled with the analytical insights and the keen perceptive spirit of Dr. Outler to the working of the Holy Spirit in this day. These lectures achieved what many who heard them delivered were to call "a monumental contribution."

Theology in the Wesleyan Spirit is described by Bishop William R. Cannon as follows:

> *Dr. Outler, in expounding Wesley's theology, like a dutiful disciple, has successfully imitated the Master's example. His book is clear and simple as well as elegantly composed. His reading public is the common lot of Christian people in the English speaking world. One does not have to be tutored in theology to understand and appreciate the theology he here sets forth.*
>
> *This book is another gem in the crown of his gifted contributions to Wesleyan theology and is a noble tribute to the enduring quality of Mr. Wesley's theology. Methodists and non-Methodists alike can profit from this little book.*

EDITOR'S NOTE: Albert Outler's texts of *Evangelism in the Wesleyan Spirit* and *Theology in the Wesleyan Spirit* were prepared for different audiences with different expectations. The *Evangelism* text is less formal with few reference notes while the *Theology* text is more scholarly with extensive reference notes. Both will be of value to the reader.

Dr. Outler's text, as well as his quotations from the writings of John Wesley and others, have been left in their original form. Both Dr. Outler and John Wesley wrote and lived in eras when gender-inclusive language was neither norm nor practice.

The lectures contained herein are based on the Denman Lectureship in Evangelism, which were established to honor the life and ministry of Dr. Harry Denman, retired General Secretary of the General Board of Evangelism of the former Methodist Church. These lectures were delivered at the United Methodist Congress on Evangelism meeting in New Orleans, Louisiana in January, 1971.

Library of Congress Catalog Card Number: 72171886

Evangelism
in the Wesleyan Spirit

I: Wesley the Evangelist

bviously, it is going to be important for all of us, in our time together here in this great Congress, to be as open and honest as possible. So I might as well begin by confessing to you frankly that I was mildly startled to be invited to deliver these Denman Lectures – as some of you may have been by the news that I had accepted the assignment. I'm certainly not the first person I would have thought of for such a job – an aging academic, with no special talent for rousements, with a lifelong dedication to the substance of Christian orthodoxy but within the "liberal" tradition, with no special affinity for much of what has passed for "evangelism" in our church. What are *his* credentials? – and my only point in raising such a question is to indicate that if any of you have raised that question (or may raise it before we are through here), you are not alone.

But maybe what matters more are my reasons for accepting the invitation, and for accounting this occasion as a great honor and an exciting challenge. On this score, I am quite clear and confident. In the first place, it is a welcome opportunity to add my own personal tribute, along with yours, to the life and work of Harry Denman – a grateful act of sincere praise and thanksgiving for a great man and a great career. Dr. Denman and my father were friends and mutual admirers for many years and I, too, have cherished his contributions to the Christian cause over the years. In my generation, no man in Methodism has made a wider or deeper spiritual impact on the Methodist church, or through it. If, therefore, these lectures may serve in any meaningful way to extend and reinforce that influence, it will have been a privilege to do so.

But then, in the second place, I thought I saw how they might provide an opportunity to reach still further back in our heritage, in an appeal to the mind and heart of yet another great evangelist, John Wesley, and claim for ourselves whatever is still living and pertinent in his life and work that, in an earlier age, stirred yet another great faltering, demoralized church (like ours today) to unexpected renewal. For years, now, I have nurtured this stubborn hope that if, in the church that still honors him as hero and mentor, we could grasp the essence of his legacy and suitably update it in our time and place, we too might see something of the marvels of the Spirit vouchsafed to Wesley and to the church of his day. Such as they may be, therefore, these lectures are dedicated in grateful memory to two of my favorite people – without nostalgia but still with the earnest hope that their legacies may prove more relevant for tomorrow than some of us have ever yet realized.

And yet, even if my intentions in these lectures are clear enough and honorable, the lectures themselves have been something of an agony in their preparing – and may still be in their delivery and hearing. They have little or nothing to do with any salvation (as I understand *that!*), but they have been wrought out with real fear and trembling. "Evangelism," in the Methodist tradition, has acquired a typical theological cast and disposition that I do not fully share. Many of its stereotypes have struck me as one-sided and exclusivist and, worst of all, many of its characteristic negations have seemed to me to breach the law of forbearance and charity. By the same token, however, I feel no guaranteed right to a sympathetic and positive hearing in a company such as this. I must speak my mind and heart as openly and honestly as I can; you must be as open and honest in your response. My only hope is that we have already agreed, in principle, as to our common court of appeals: Holy Scripture, the Wesleyan tradition, and the crucible of living faith in Jesus Christ as Savior and Lord. Convict me of error before these judges and you can lead me to repentance. Otherwise, the wisest way is to follow Wesley's advice to his people in the case of disputed questions: "to think and let think."

One of the commonplace rituals in church meetings of all sorts nowadays is a vivid requiem for these raddled times and the church's dire perils. I certainly do not mean to deny that the times are raddled or that the church is in dire peril. I am assuming, rather, that you are already familiar with one or another version of such a ritual, and so, in the interest of time, I'd like to move directly to three of the specific aspects in the current crisis that bear most nearly on our contemporary concerns and on the future prospects for Christian evangelism.

The first of these is a widespread and spreading demoralization throughout the churches, at every level and in every sector. There is an obvious and ominous loss of nerve and poise amongst a great multitude of those who call and profess themselves Christian. Even the most self-assured and militant amongst us (whether self-styled "evangelicals" or the self-anointed "prophets of revolution") sound more strident and abrasive than truly confident or convincing. The laity are in unaccustomed ferment, the rank-and-file clergy are quietly desperate, our leaders are more badgered and bewildered than they can afford to admit. Seminarians are being whipsawed between rival demands that they *learn* something (e.g. the intellectual substance of the Christian tradition) and that they *do* something (e.g. help usher in the Kingdom here and now). Extremists from both left and right have learned that the churches can be intimidated or embarrassed – but have not yet learned how to turn their dubious victories into anything resembling real renewal.

Alongside this crisis of morale, and correlated with it, is the beginning of a wholesale defection of the middle class and the young from their traditional roles in American Christianity, without comparable replacement from the ranks of labor or the intelligentsia – or for that matter, from those disadvantaged groups on whose behalf the church has rightly risked the alienation of her bourgeois clientele. The gathering storm predicted by Geoffrey Hadden – the polarizations between "evangelicals" and "activists," between "liberal" clergy and "conservative" laymen, the rifts between young and old, between blacks and whites, between "middle-America" and the "countercultures," etc. – this gathering storm has already struck, with no signs of abatement any time soon. All this is reflected in the downward tilt of the quantitative measures of institutional prosperity: loyalty, support, participation. A new global climate of furious discontent has come to permeate all our institutions: the church *and* the academy *and* the body politic.

Moreover, it is merely forlorn to hope that this is just a momentary episode in some larger scheme of human progress that utopia is still ahead and available on passionate demand; or, alternatively, that we can turn the clock back to any good old days (such as *they* were!) simply by repeating their rhetoric and replicating their methods. For, in the third place, the deepest root of our current crisis is a radical mutation occurring in the depths of the human consciousness of modern man. Its most obvious surface manifestations may be recognized in the weakening of all the old taboos and compulsions that have served Western society (and Christian culture) as moral control systems for millennia, the radical dissolution of old linkages between psychological anxiety and religious guilt, the swift fading of the church's moral influence in contemporary society insofar as that influence is based on any claims to arbitrary and external authority. The collapse of these customary moral controls (what Freud called the super-ego or what William Graham Sumner called "the tyranny of social mores") is everywhere evident, but its import for theology and preaching has not yet been fully grasped. Modern men are as anxious as ever – even more so, what with the escalating pressures of modern existence – but they are rarely as guilt-ridden as we know our ancestors to have been, and what guilt they feel is rarely related to their awareness of *God's* relentless judgment against *sin*. The discontent of the disaffected is typically vented on "those others" – the Establishment, or the heretics, or the new left, or the new right, or whatever. Repentance comes hard to the self-righteous – and we are being drowned in a flood of self-righteousness, from all sides and of all sorts!

All of this affects evangelism, and our understanding of evangelism – if by evangelism we mean the communication of the gospel and the maturation of Christians in the community of the church and in the human community at large. How can a halfhearted church sing, "True-hearted, whole-hearted, etc.," and still hope to catch the attention either of the dispirited, or even of the bigots of this world? How can a dispirited church renew her "life in the Spirit"? How can a polarized church persuade men of her "one Lord, one faith, one baptism"? How can a church that once relied on guilt-ridden consciences to bring men to the threshold of conversion hope to pinch the moral nerve of what is actually a new breed of antinomians?

If evangelism means God's good news to man's bad news, then its success always depends on how this message is understood and interpreted and applied. And because there is, obviously, a massive confusion and disagreement in the Christian community at just this very point, I have felt emboldened to turn back, in the Christian heritage, for perspective and insight that may come from another age. And when I do, John Wesley seems such an obvious choice, because of the striking similarities between his concerns and ours, and also because I believe that in his theory and practice of Christian evangelism there is a perennial vitality still available.

This first lecture, therefore, will try to interpret Wesley as the evangelist that he was; the second will focus on his understanding of the fundamentals of the Christian evangel and the nature of Christian communication and communion. In the third lecture, taking a cue from Wesley's own futuristic outlook, we shall speculate on the prospects for a "*Third* Great Awakening" in the last quarter of this twentieth century – a revival that might move us beyond the stereotypes of evangelism formed in the Great Awakenings of the eighteenth and nineteenth centuries and that, for many, still define the essence of evangelism. Then, finally, in the fourth, casting caution to the winds, I should like to share with you a blurred vision of mine: a church of Spirit-filled martyrs and servants, a church that would be evangelical in action as well as proclamation, and not just evangelical, either, but catholic and reformed as well.

In appealing to John Wesley like this, there is no use holding him up as an example that any of us should seek blindly to imitate. For it is one of the more intriguing ironies of history that if John Wesley had died at any time before his thirty-sixth birthday (17 June, 1739 – a full twelve months *after* Aldersgate), his name would not rate a footnote in the history books. Consider his situation in the spring of 1739. He had been elected to a prestigious fellowship in Oxford with an ample stipend and few regular duties, but he had decided against returning to Oxford after the fiasco of his missionary venture in Georgia. For he had failed as a teacher and had earned a reputation for "being a little crackbrained" (Journal, II, 243). He had been leader of a religious society in Oxford, another such society in Georgia, still a third in London – with no visible or lasting effects in any of them. He had hammered out the substance of a sound theology that would stand stable all his life and had published it in a little theological manifesto (1738) that had stirred no ripples, as yet. A bold critic of the Establishment, he had few political instincts and no power base. Moreover, he had been converted – not once, but twice (in Oxford in 1725, and in London, in 1738). He had spent a summer in the German strongholds of Moravian piety and was currently locked in a bitter struggle with the Moravian quietists in the society at Fetter Lane. He was an evangelical, all right – orthodox in doctrine, zealous in personal faith, self-righteous and overweening – but with next to nothing to show for thirty-six full years of high-minded diligence. How many of us would have hung in there so long with such a meager harvest? Wesley might not have either if it had not been for his income from his Lincoln College fellowship. Indeed, one might meditate on the irony of the fact that the opening decade of the Methodist Revival was actually financed by Lincoln College.

And yet, a decade later, this little man had emerged at the head of the most effective mass movement in eighteenth century England – a great upwelling of Christian faith and of social reform as well. He had finally pulled out of the society in Fetter Lane and had founded yet another one, this time his very own. He had formed his lay preachers into an "Annual Conference" – concerned chiefly with doctrine and morale! – and had become the chief theological tutor to the Methodist people (with a constant flow of sermons, hymns and tracts for their study and edification). He had shaken the Establishment to its foundations without a single contestation – and had found new ways to channel and conserve immense spiritual forces being unleashed in the Revival.

Don't ask me for a manipulative formula for this success – and don't take Wesley for your model, whatever your other current ambitions. He was an obsessive-compulsive neurotic all his life and his religion never really cured his neurosis. He had an authoritarian temper – all too often imitated, without comparable results. Aldersgate had warmed his heart but had not taught him how to communicate the gospel or how to guide men into holiness. What, then, are we to make of this strange, late-blooming heralding of Christ – this unprogrammed outpouring of the Holy Spirit?

There is a mystery here that I don't pretend to understand – but there are also some important aspects of this transformation from barren to fruit-bearing evangelism that can be analyzed and that might be relevant to our concerns here in this Congress. The first of these was Wesley's conversion from passion to *com*passion as his dominant emotion, his change from a harsh zealot of God's judgment to a winsome witness to God's grace, from a censorious critic to an effective pastor, from arrogance to humility.

The sign-event of this remarkable conversion – not its cause, else we could duplicate his results simply by adopting his methods – was Wesley's embarrassed descent into field preaching on 2 April, 1739. This was an even more decisive event for the Revival than Aldersgate although, of course, without Aldersgate, *this* would scarcely have been possible. In any case, it was a shattering experience for the Oxford don who had hitherto cared so much more about "delivering his own soul" than about the needs and dispositions of other people.

> *Monday, 2 – At four in the afternoon I submitted to be more vile and proclaimed in the highways the glad tidings of salvation, speaking from a little eminence in the ground adjoining to the city to about three thousand people. The scripture on which I spoke (is it possible any one should be ignorant that it is fulfilled in every true minister of Christ?) was, "The Spirit of the Lord is upon me, because He hath anointed me to preach the gospel to the poor. He hath sent me to heal the broken-hearted; to preach deliverance to the captives, and recovery of sight to the blind; to set at liberty them that are bruised, to proclaim the acceptable year of the Lord."*
>
> *(Journal, II, 172-73)*

This was obviously not the first time that Wesley had preached "the glad tidings of salvation," but it was almost the first time that anybody else had really *heard* these tidings for themselves in *his* preaching of them. And part of this must have been because here his proclamation had finally passed over from highly self-conscious words to truly unself-conscious action. His passion for truth had been transformed into compassion for persons. This visible demonstration of his actual identification with them had stirred forlorn men to a real "hearing of faith," and it was *their* hearing of faith that finally clinched Wesley's firm grasp upon his own faith. It was Wesley's belated success as an evangelist that finally made him into an assured believer.

This might well remind us that the gospel is not truly preached until it has been truly heard. Zeal, passion, rhetorical overkill – none of these, nor all of them together, constitute the secret of effective evangelism. "Preach faith until *you* have it" had been Peter Böhler's prescription, but it hadn't worked out like that. Instead, Wesley had preached faith until *others* had it – and *that* was what broke the drought in his own spirit.

From Mr. Wesley's published sermons it is not always readily apparent how and why his oral preaching had the impact on people that we know it had. But you must remember that those published sermons were written out chiefly for the use of members in the Methodist societies – less for their conversion to Christ than for their doctrinal instruction in Christian truth and living. In the oral preaching ("about 800 sermons in a year . . . .") Wesley's primary aim seems always to have been contact, impact, decision – all in the atmosphere of a vivid personal concern and graciousness. Consider, for example, some of the favorite texts of his oral preaching:

1. Ephesians 2:8 – "For by grace are ye saved through faith; and that not of yourselves: it is the gift of God."
2. Mark 1: 15 – ". . . Repent ye and believe the gospel."
3. 1 Cor. 1:30 – "But of him are ye in Christ Jesus, who of God is made unto us wisdom, and righteousness, and sanctification, and redemption."
4. Isaiah 55:6 – "Seek ye the Lord while he may be found; call ye upon him while he is near."
5. Ezekiel 33 :11 – "Say unto them, As I live, saith the Lord God, I have no pleasure in the death of the wicked; but that the wicked turn from his way and live: turn ye, turn ye from your evil ways; for why will ye die, O house of Israel?"
6. Hosea 14:4 – "I will heal their backsliding, I will love them freely: for mine anger is turned away from him."
7. Matthew 16:26 – "For what is a man profited, if he shall gain the whole world, and lose his own soul or what shall a man give in exchange for his soul?"
8. Acts 16:30 – ". . . What must I do to be saved?"

Now, only *three* of these endlessly repeated texts appear in the 150 published sermons, from which one may infer that Wesley's *oral* preaching was dominated by his effort to come close to people with the message of God's seeking, importunate love, whereas his *published* sermons were a parallel effort to lead men and women into a clearer understanding of their faith and a more faithful response to the divine imperatives in their Christian existence.

Wesley became an effective evangelist when he was finally enabled, by grace, to offer himself to his hearers as an importunate herald and servant of God – rather than flinging the gospel at them like a soteriological brickbat. It was this grace of compassion – the compassion of Christ's self-giving love – that transformed a thirty-six year old zealot into the father of the people called Methodists. One might wonder in passing if there is a lesson here for some of us – even those past thirty-six?

Another aspect of Wesley's newfound success was his firm conviction that conversion is never more than the bare threshold of authentic and comprehensive evangelism. Most of his hearers were already church members of one sort or another. What they needed was new depth and dimension in their nominal Christian professions. Sometimes, this meant "preaching Christ" in judgment on their self-righteousness. Sometimes, it meant "preaching Christ" in mercy on their despair. But always, "preaching Christ" was aimed beyond confession and conversion toward the fullness of faith and the endless maturing of life in grace. "Follow the blow," said he, "never encourage the devil by snatching souls from him that you cannot nurture." "Converts without nurture are like still-born babies." Thus, the evangelist accepted a continued responsibility for his converts' growth in grace; thus, sanctification became the goal and end of all valid evangelistic endeavor (and this implies a lifelong process).

Now, how did profession of faith and enrollment in the church's membership – i.e. nominal Christianity! – ever come to be an end in itself in our own conventional notions of evangelism? It never was for Wesley. Obviously, conversions, professions, enrollment, attendance, financial support are all urgent and important aspects of any truly fruitful evangelism. But how did we drift into the absurd situation where "evangelism" is associated almost exclusively with the initial stages of Christian existence, "Christian education" with its ongoing processes, "missions" with its global outreach and "Christian social concerns" with its impact on the world – all of these with different theological attitudes and often with competing claims on the church's fealty and support? Wesley had a horror of men who professed themselves Christian but who could not communicate their faith through the witness of their words and lives – that is to say, church members who are not living witnesses to Christ in the service of their brethren.

For Wesley, the scope of evangelism was never less than the fullness of Christian experience – "holiness of heart, and a life conformable to the same" – and he never faltered in this insistence, even when his societies began to bulge and Methodism began to be respectable. Is this also our understanding of the meaning and scope of evangelism in our time and circumstances? If not, why not?

There is still another aspect of Wesley's evangelistic program that very much needs emphasis – especially because it was so largely lost sight of by later generations of Methodists in America. For Wesley, the essence of faith was personal and inward, but the evidence of faith was public and social. "It is expected of all those who continue in these Societies that they shall continue to *evidence* their desire of salvation – first, by doing no harm, such as . . .; second, by doing all the good they can, such as . . .; and third, by attending upon all the ordinances of God, such as . . ." [I'd be interested to know how many of you instantly recognized this citation from the General Rules which have always stood in our *Discipline* and which our pastors were supposed to read and expound annually in the congregations – until the General Conference of 1968 dropped that requirement in a fit of absent-mindedness.]

My point is that evangelism must issue in visible social effects or else its fruits will fade and wither. Christian proclamation must take on visible form and the Christian community must be committed to social reform, or else it will stultify our Lord's prayer that God's righteous will shall be done *on earth* – here and now, in justice and love and peace – as always it is being done in heaven. Outward witness in daily living is the necessary confirmation of any inward experience of inward faith. The Word made *audible* must become the Word made *visible*, if men's lives are ever to be touched by the "Word made flesh."

With this end in view, Wesley gathered his converts into societies – and related them to the sacraments of the church, on the one hand, and to a process of Christian discipline and shared "life in the Spirit," on the other. Out of this process he raised up a growing company of lay witnesses for Christ. This was not a stage *beyond* evangelism. It was, rather, the evangelistic enterprise itself in its natural unfolding; for Wesley understood, as we seem to have forgotten, that it is the Word *made visible* in the lives of practicing, witnessing lay Christians that constitutes the church's most powerful evangelistic influence.

In one sense of the word, Mr. Wesley was the Methodist Revival incarnate in one man – he was the personal autocrat of "those in connexion with Mr. Wesley." But in a far profounder sense, it was the Methodist laymen who made Mr. Wesley's evangelistic career the success that it was. There were other evangelists in the eighteenth century and some of them (like George Whitefield) had more converts to their personal credit. But John Wesley had somehow grasped the secret of the Word made social, and of the faith that works by love not only in the heart but in the world as well. And this, as we can see in his case, makes the crucial difference between a sort of "evangelism" that scores repeated triumphs that pass and fade and an evangelical reform movement that leaves a permanent deposit in the church and in the world.

For Wesley organized his converts into societies, with rules and rituals, with programs of self-directed nurture and with a lay leadership that was locally responsible, along with and often in spite of his overall autocratic supervision. Generally speaking – and this is my main point here – he left the local societies largely on their own. For the greater part of any given year, it was the Methodist laymen who were the most visible exemplars of evangelical Christianity in any given local community; *they* were the actual sponsors of the Revival, the real martyrs for Christ at the grassroots level. And over the years, this was the vital complement to Mr. Wesley's own zealous preaching and his journeyings over the land. The result was that an authoritarian leader managed to raise up an institution that was monarchical in form and yet actually democratic in much of its grassroots operation – a system that gave men and women experiences of vital Christian fellowship and responsible local leadership.

Evangelism has always stressed the Word made audible, the Word made personal, and all that. "How can they have faith in whom they have never heard; and how can they hear without a preacher? . . . We conclude [said Paul] that faith is awakened by preaching and that the preaching that awakens faith comes through the Word of Christ." (Romans 10:14-17). In and through the Methodist societies, however, the Word made audible was also made visible and thus became even more effective, as the societies became evangelistic agencies in their own right. Thousands of men and women who may never have heard Wesley preach (or only on rare occasions) were attracted to the Christian life and were actually evangelized (converted, born again, nurtured and matured) by the outreaching and ingathering influence of the local Methodist people. It was not only their preaching that made its impact in the world but also their lives – on the job, in the marketplace, in their redemptive involvement in the social agonies of their times. And no matter what stage a convert's Christian experience might have reached, his life in the society and class meetings was always aimed at the way beyond, and he could count on guidance and help along that way – all the way to "perfection in love in this life." George Eliot's "Adam Bede" was converted by Methodist lay witness – by a woman at that! – an interesting testimony to the widespread conviction amongst English social reformers (George Eliot was not a professing Christian but rather a humanistic social reformer) that evangelism for the Wesleyans was more than conversion and regeneration. It was, instead, both initiation and maturation in Christ and in Christian fellowship – and an implicit, indirect, social revolution.

Early Methodism was a lay witness movement with all the crudities and excesses that go with such things. But Wesley had come to realize (against all his clerical instincts) that it is the laity who *are* the church visible in the world. It is the laity who bear the Name of Christ into the shops and marketplaces of the world. It is the laity who are his martyrs and servants (witnesses, in life and death, to God's outpoured and outpouring love).

God's good news is proclaimed in words and symbols, it is celebrated in liturgies and rituals, but it is communicated by corporate life and example. In this mysterious transaction, the ordained and representative clergy have a crucial role, in Word and sacrament and order, in sacral and pastoral leadership and enablement. They, too, are evangelists, of course, but the church's evangelistic mission is still, first and last, a lay enterprise: God's love lived out in the daily round – in the *saeculum* – God's imperatives to justice and human dignity translated into service and self-denying love. This was Wesley's motto for the first Methodist societies – and it could also be our clue to a more fully valid and fruitful evangelism in our time and in our future.

There was a further social dimension to Mr. Wesley's concern for personal religion and for lay witness – which is to say, a new kind of man with a new kind of Christian self-consciousness and a new political conscience. The English proletariat of Wesley's day were locked into a servile social system, replete with distinctions of superiority and inferiority, etc., etc. It was a disorderly society and a fiercely oppressive one, as we know very well from *The Beggars' Opera, Moll Flanders, Tom Jones*, etc., etc.

Wesley was not a conscious rebel against this society as such and so never set himself to overturn it directly. But he had an uncommon confidence in the common man and he was also careful to keep his preachers constantly on the move, so that local Methodists rarely took their self-images from any individual preacher, not even Mr. Wesley. From Methodist preaching, men and women heard about God's high evaluation of their own human dignity – of the love that motivated the Incarnation and accepted the Cross. And then, in the weekly rounds of the Methodist societies, they experienced this special dignity in newly personal circumstances, new experiences of peer-group equality – with real group involvement and actual social responsibility.

What happened, as we can now see in retrospect, was revolutionary in actual fact and consequence. Such men and women found themselves sloughing off their shackles of servility, and becoming the available leadership cadre for one of the most effective, least disruptive social revolutions on record. They emerged as a new class – men and women with a new dignity conferred on them, not by birth or wealth or power, but by God and their Christian brethren. And this gave economic and political muscle for a whole succession of significant social reforms (the trades union movement, prison reform, the abolition of slavery, etc., etc.). Halevy's famous comment that Methodism saved England from the French Revolution missed the point almost altogether. What the Revival did was to sponsor a very different kind of revolution – an actual transformation of social morals and manners, the partial meaning of which we can measure when we compare the human lot in the England of 1750 with that of 1850 (still far from perfect but infinitely improved) or if we compare England and America in 1850 and now in our own 1971. Here, then, we have an edifying paradox: an evangelist who was a political conservative (many of them have been – many still are today!) shaping and loosing a powerful agency for social change, a movement that was evangelical and reformist at one and the same time – and all of this on the premise of the freedom and dignity of the Christian man whose love of his neighbor is a vital function of his love of God.

Wesley's program as an evangelist combined an evangelical view of Christian existence (the vertical dimension of God's sovereign grace in Christ) with a catholic understanding of Christian nurture and maturation (a real and relative righteousness that looks toward perfection in love in this life, that excludes all human utopias and perfection-*isms*). He wanted to prepare men and women for the daily triumphs of grace but always within a corporate matrix of disciplined fellowship. He knew – as we keep forgetting – that men shall not live by bread alone nor yet without bread; not by violence but also not in servility and destitution; not by institutional self-maintenance nor yet without institutions. He had discovered – as we must rediscover – that evangelism barely begins with conversion and a profession of faith, that it must always lead beyond to a lifelong mission of witness and service in the world for which Christ died.

And this is why the Wesleyan style of proclamation and nurture strikes me as newly relevant – why his conception of Christian experience as a distinctive way of life rooted in the love of God and love of neighbor and expressed in meaningful social action guided by neighborly love is still a clue to any program for renewal in the contemporary church that will not in fact corrupt it. It was Wesley's confidence in God that saved him from overweening self-confidence. It was his radical trust in the righteousness of Christ that saved him from self-righteousness. It was his vision of the human possibility, his active caring for persons and for human society that saved Wesley from despair or smugness. And, finally, it was his insistence on the Word made *visible* — in life and society — that saved him and his movement from the swift oblivion into which most evangelistic triumphs have a way of slipping.

The days of authentic evangelism are not over. The ebbing tides will flow again; new Pentecosts are already in the making. But they will not come in the course of "business as usual," nor yet by any simplistic reliance on the stereotypes that have passed for "evangelical" and "evangelistic." It is the Wesleyan *spirit* that we must pray and hope for once again: that strange miracle that turned a censorious zealot into a herald of grace, that fusion of mind and heart and muscle in joyful service, that move from passion to *compassion*, that linkage of revival *and* reform, that stress on *local initiative* within a connexional system — that actual willingness to live in and to be led by the Spirit of God in faith and hope and love.

This is our legacy. This is what God wrought in and through this forefather of ours in the faith. But it is also God's clear call to us in the here and now — his insistence that we should repossess it for ourselves and others, that we should give it new relevance in a new world: a world in travail for a new humanity. He that hath ears to hear, let him hear!

Mo-Nophy-site — one who maintains the anti-Chalcedonian doctrine that the human & divine in the person of JX constitute only one nature — compare - Armenian

Dyophysite. Chalcedonian doctrine that full deity & full humanity exist in the person of JX - 2 natures w/o confusion or change

II: Wesley's Evangel

ords like *evangel, evangelical, evangelism* have an honored history. They point to the heart of the gospel – the *evangelion*, "the glad tidings of our salvation," the marvelous good news that God has met our deepest needs and highest hopes in and through Jesus Christ. *Evangelion* – the story of Jesus and the new quality of existence in which all men may share, a new style of life of love and service in and for the world.

But these fine old words have also generated many a distorted image in many modern minds – abrasive zealots flinging their Bibles about like missiles, men (and sometimes women!) with a flat earth theology, a monophysite Christology, a montanist ecclesiology and a psychological profile suggestive of hysteria. Every Saturday night in *The Dallas Times-Herald* there are advertisements for these characters – eyes ablaze, bodies coiled for the leap of faith, or for pouncing on the hapless sinner. Occasionally, we have gatherings of self-styled "evangelicals" who have much needful truth to speak, alongside many uncharitable remarks about other Christians. Last summer, it was announced to a large and lively convocation that our United Methodist Church seminary faculties would bear watching because some of their members "profess no faith in God, doubt his existence, regard Jesus as only a good man – not a Savior – have no place for prayer, etc., etc." It was not said who or where or how many such apostates there are; it was a blanket indictment. And this is my point. For even if we allow for a tiny fraction of truth in this indiscriminate libel, it still fails to endear the evangelical cause to fair-minded men.

What it does is to remind us that this acrid image of the typical "evangelical" is no mere illusion. Run a psychological analysis on any clutch of ranters, on the one side, and an equal number of effective fruit-bearing heralds of Christ, on the other, and some interesting generalizations emerge. The difference between the two groups is often not in doctrine as such, nor in their psychological profiles, nor even in their zeal in the Lord's service – but rather in the presence or absence of a quality of soul best labeled "gracious" or "grace-filled." I ran such a study once on an interesting octet of truly great evangelists – Paul, Luther, Ignatius Loyola, George Whitefield, John Wesley, Francis Asbury, Charles Finney, and Billy Graham. One of the more obvious parallels between all these men was a striking similarity in psychological character. All appeared to share a high-pituitary syndrome; their native instincts ran toward aggression and manipulation; all are the heroes in their own best illustrations; all share what psychologists nowadays label as "the authoritarian personality." In every case, but for the grace of God and the partial redemption of their power-drives, "obnoxious" would have been an accurate enough designation of their respective dispositions.

This suggests that the difference between healthy and unhealthy evangelism has less to do with the fervor of a man's faith or the pure truth of his doctrines than with the quality of his love for others – his transparent respect for human dignity in every single manifestation of it. The authentic evangelical has what John Wesley commended as "catholic spirit" – an openness of heart and mind that cherishes diversity within the larger unity of essential faith and commitment.

The essential fallacy in all unhealthy evangelism – in all its varieties – is its hidden strategy of *self*-justification, masked by the flaming rhetoric of radical faith. Do you want to be saved? Do you want to go to heaven? Do you want to be ready when Jesus comes again? Are you eager to flee from the wrath to come, while others perish in their sins? O.K.: then latch onto the right doctrine, for believing *that* is a meritorious good work. Check off the seven steps to salvation (or is it nine or twelve?); take 'em, in the right order, and you've got it made. Or (the same strategy in obverse), do you seek "peace of mind" or "authentic self-consciousness"? Here's a formula for plugging into the divine power supply that will operate your own psychic appliances! Do you want law and order? Or, would you rather have liberation, justice, and peace? No matter. Get God on your side – or at least make the unhesitating claim that God is on your side and that your cause is his cause!

But this points us to another fine line of distinction, for the *evan-*

gelion says plainly that God *is* on our side — that "for us men and our salvation, Christ came down from heaven and was incarnate by the Holy Spirit of Mary the Virgin — *and was made man!*" In and through the charisms of the Spirit, divine power *does* become operative in our hearts and lives. God's purposes for his children — *all* his children — *do* include freedom, righteousness, peace, and joy in the Spirit. But all of this on *his* terms, at *his* initiative. It is not our part to control the dynamic equilibrium between God's grace and man's response, but rather to find and lose ourselves in participation in the divine-human relationship in which God acts and man reacts. The less self-conscious our faith, the less self-righteous our assurance of God's healing love. Something like this is the gist of the doctrine of justification by faith alone, with no antecedent merit whatsoever.

John Wesley came finally to understand this "grand doctrine," as he called it, as the axis of his entire doctrinal system. He never really believed in salvation by good works, but he had flirted long and fruitlessly with the hope that orthodox doctrine, fervent devotion, stringent self-discipline and zealous good works might, all together, earn him some measure of divine favor — or at least might mitigate the divine wrath against him. Finally, he was driven to the discovery that it is by faith alone (radical, buoyant trust) that self-righteousness is displaced by the righteousness of Christ. By faith — and faith alone! — uptight lives are relaxed, trapped lives liberated, arrogant lives humbled, soiled lives cleansed, slouching lives raised up to tiptoe, empty lives filled, life unto death turned into life unto life.

And so, with all his probings of their sin, Wesley offered his hearers repentance and pardoning love. With all his plumbing of their despair and guilt, he promised them the lively hope of God's accepting love. With every shattering of their claims to self-righteousness (orthodoxy, church membership, mystical experience, etc.), he hastened to stress the mystery of God's free grace — pardon that depends on nothing man can do or be, but rather on what God has done for us and promised us in Jesus Christ. This is justifying faith. This is the act of trust that lays trustful claim to God's offer of love. This is the faith that works by love and that issues in a life of moral strenuousness. Justification is the threshold of a faith-relationship that looks beyond itself toward its fullness: which is to say, "holiness of heart and life." For Wesley, evangelism was the communication of the *evangelion*: the whole story of God's gracious dealings with man over the whole range of human existence and yet also the appropriation of the *evangelion*, in a life that is a new creation in Christ.

He often insisted that he wanted no part of doctrinal novelty or innovation.

> Methodism, so called, is the old religion, the religion of the
> Bible, the religion of the primitive church, the religion of the
> Church of England. This old religion . . . is no other than
> love, the love of God and of all mankind . . . This love is
> the great medicine of life . . . Wherever this is, there are virtue
> and happiness going hand in hand . . . This religion of love
> and joy and peace has its seat in the inmost soul; but is ever
> showing itself by its fruits . . . spreading virtue and happi-
> ness all around it.

But if Wesley was fully conscious of his commitment to the great central tradition of Christian faith and understanding, he felt entirely free to adapt and develop his own contemporary modes of interpretation and communication of the gospel. He was confident that most professing Christians could mark off "the marrow of Christian truth" and he thought that he could specify this common core of sound doctrine – not in a single definitive statement but in many approximate summaries.

For example, in the sermon on "Catholic Spirit," Wesley lays out the Christian basics on which all Christians agree, as he supposes: (1) faith in God and his providence, experienced by a "supernatural conviction"; (2) faith in Jesus Christ, "God over all, blessed forever, revealed in the [human] soul, formed in the heart by faith"; (3) the love of God casting out the love of the world; (4) a life committed to God's will, aiming only at God's glory; (5) the hope of "a conscience void of offence toward God and toward man"; (6) the love of neighbor with visible evidence of that love in daily life. Given this much, he was prepared not merely to tolerate but actually to welcome theological, liturgical, and psychological differences across a broad spectrum.

In his open *Letter to a Roman Catholic* (1749), he formulated a compact "confession of faith," to prove that he and his separated Catholic brethren share common doctrinal ground and that although their disagreements are still very real, these disagreements ought not to preclude their mutual recognition and fraternal love in Christ. Wesley's impromptu "confession" follows the classical three-articled form (Father, Son and Holy Spirit). It consists of ten basic doctrinal affirmations and is followed by a description of the Christian life that is the expected fruit of such a faith. Allowing for the requisite task of translating Wesley's rhetoric into twentieth century notions, I'd be willing to have you check your orthodoxy, and mine, by this remarkable, and intentionally ecumenical, "credo." There are other such summaries as well – in *An Earnest Appeal* (1743), several of the sermons and letters, etc.

What all of this shows is that Wesley set no store by the specific rhetoric of his various doctrinal formularies. This positive affinity for theological flexibility is seen in his choice of a set of *sermons* and *exegetical notes* as doctrinal guidelines for his preachers rather than anything more rigid or exclusivist. The *Sermons*, taking them all together, add up to his *summa theologica* – but they also demonstrate the versatility of his theological repertoire. The mystery of God in Christ through the Spirit is central. No single conceptual system can ever exhaust this mystery, or drive all interpretations from the field. Thus, interpretations of this mystery are of necessity partial and plural – and this is rather the strength of the faith than any weakness in it.

Wesley was equally averse to one-sided and rigid norms of doctrinal authority. Scripture, of course, stood first and foremost for him; "the oracles of God are the original charter of Christianity." But *sola Scripture* did not mean "nothing but Scripture." Wesley read Scripture through the eyes of tradition; he tested its insights in the crucible of personal experience and he sought to understand them within the strictures of reason. Of all affirmations – his own and others – he demanded that they be rooted in the Bible, illumined by tradition, realized in experience and confirmed by reason – all together, none apart from the others. This is why a Methodist has actually abandoned the Wesleyan tradition if and when he turns biblic*ist*, or traditional*ist*, or existential*ist*, or rational*ist*. He has also repudiated Wesley's "catholic spirit" when he starts berating, or excommunicating, others for views or practices that do not contradict the Christian basics.

John Wesley's evangelism was, by conscious intent and careful reflection, neither more nor less than "the faith once for all delivered to the saints" – mind you, not delivered in any special package of formularies nor in any single doctrinal system, nor in terms of a single specific worldview or any actual political frame. The *evangelion* is perennial, but its interpretation is forever in development. Theological reflection is an endless, mutable process. *Semper reformanda* applies not only to church polity and structure, but to doctrine and liturgy and ethos as well. A church continues to be evangelical only by being constantly and unanxiously reformed – and this means change – constant updating, constant new ventures, as history and human destinies unfold. The People of God are a Pilgrim People. The Holy City is forever receding on history's horizons.

But if Wesley stood self-consciously in the central tradition of catholic Christianity, there is something quite distinctive in his particular configuration and synthesis of the great Christian themes: faith *and* good works, Scripture *and* tradition, God's sovereignty *and* human freedom, universal grace *and* conditional election, original sin *and* Christian perfection. The only opinions he ever condemned outright were those that denigrated Scripture, or that threatened the vital balance between justification and sanctification, or that excluded other allowable interpretations. An example of this was Whitefield's insistence on predestination to the exclusion of any substantive emphasis on moral agency.

In many ways, however, the most original aspect of Wesley's evangel was his concept of the *humanum* – his rather special vision of the human possibility in the economy of grace. I'd like to comment on this briefly, for it has a vital bearing on what I understand to be a distinctive Methodist emphasis in evangelism and in the whole range of doctrine and life. This vision of Christian existence begins with "the hearing of faith" – the moment of actual conversion. The man who finally hears God's good news for him is one who, beforehand, was either desperate or empty or smug. He was, as Wesley said, "dead" or, at best, an "*almost* Christian." The gist of sin is man's false perception of God's wrath, or of his mercy, or of his absence. The sinner supposes himself as either able to save himself (which is false) or else as hopelessly lost (which is also false). The transit from the death of sin to the life of faith is made possible by the disclosure, in Christ, of God's accepting, reconciling love. The recognition and acceptance of this love as personally real is faith. And in its light, the believer recognizes himself as a new man in Christ and he begins to realize what it really means to be truly human: to be an actual *imago Dei*, a special individual creation of God – identified, sustained and consummated by divine grace. Each self is a unique mystery, inspired and sustained by God, moment by moment over life's full span – and this whether one is living in rebellion or in trust. This is what Wesley had in mind by the phrase, "prevenient grace."

In the Wesleyan evangel, the man to be evangelized exists in a lifelong, dynamic process of growth and struggle for *full*-fillment. Wesley was falsely accused by his Calvinistic critics of being virtually Pelagian.

What he was concerned with was the avoidance of the Lutheran view of man as invincibly concupiscent or the Calvinist assumptions about man's fated idolatry. The Wesleyan version of a Christian synergism begins and ends with God's sovereign grace, but it also includes man's divinely created free will, limited but real – corrupted and perverted by sin but never canceled. Wesley believed in original sin, but as a tragic malignancy rather than the actual destruction of the *imago Dei* in the sinner. He believed in total depravity (i.e. it is the man entire who is corrupted by sin, not just a part of him). But he stoutly rejected any doctrine of "tee-total depravity" (i.e. that no righteousness whatever remains in fallen man).

Human life is meaningfully related to God even in sin and estrangement; the sinner has some dim, imperfect knowledge of God in his fleeting moments of transcendental or mystical awareness; his moral conscience is deadened but not destroyed. And this is why God's prevenient grace is so crucial. It is not just that God loves us no matter what (although he does) but that his grace surrounds and anticipates us in every crisis, from birth to death, creating and holding open possibilities of growth and healing and self-fulfillment. No man is on his own, and no man can save himself or anybody else. This is the heresy of secularism, the final betrayal of man's highest hopes of becoming fully human on his own. Only in the stimulus and sustenance of God's prevenient grace is fulfillment ever possible. Wesley rules out any notion of authentic self-acceptance apart from the perception of faith. We are who we are because God made us so, because God keeps us so, and because it is God, not we, who holds open the future for our destiny – all of it by grace, unmerited, prevenient, justifying, sanctifying.

But this also means that the proclamation of the gospel presupposes the antecedent activity of the Holy Spirit in the heart of the hearer. We never speak to men who are actually ignorant of God or totally bereft of his grace. The Spirit is always there before us – and this means that our job is less that of imparting truth that would otherwise remain unknown than of stirring up the human spirit, of awakening faith – inviting and persuading men to attend to the Word within. This is why pure doctrine, as such, is less important in effecting the hearing of faith than loving witness is. This is also why formal professions of faith, as such, may mean so little – unless they also involve assurance and commitment, and unless they bear fruit in further harvests of faith, hope, and love. Our human witness in evangelism presupposes the prior witness of the Spirit in the heart – and our human witness must be consonant with the Spirit's witness or else it goes barren. The import of this distinctive view of man and God for the tasks of evangelism is crucially important.

The gospel, in Wesleyan terms, is a joyous word from God to men, through men, in the depths of their existence. It speaks of their origins and ends – of God as ground and sustenance of their existence, of man as a divine experiment in moral freedom, of man's demoralization and sin, of God in Christ reconciling the world unto himself, and of the Holy Spirit at work in a community of maturing persons. The gospel is a word of man's reliance and hope in God, of God's imperative that men should love him without stint and their neighbors without self-interest. It is a call to repentance, conversion, new life. The gospel is an invitation from the Holy Spirit to fellowship in God's beloved community, in which men are inwardly moved to outward acts of thanksgiving, worship, and service.

There is, of course, no single way in which such a message can be expressed precisely. What matters is whether we have grasped its essence both with the tendrils of our hearts and the sinews of our minds. For if we are to be persuasive heralds of Christ, we must ourselves believe the gospel that we preach. And we must match our belief with a ceaseless struggle to understand it, to communicate it, to persuade others of the truth that liberates, the love that dignifies, the peace that the world cannot give and cannot take away.

The main motifs of the Wesleyan evangel run an impressive parallel to the first principles in the Christian life as a whole: its motives, certainties, dynamics, means and ends. The prime motive of the Christian life is gratitude, our deep thankfulness and appreciation for all of God's providence and bounty, all summed up and symbolized in the saving mission of Jesus Christ. By the same token, the prime motive of evangelism is also gratitude. "I love to tell the story of Jesus and his love; . . . it did so much *for me*. . . ." The evangelist driven to his task by a sense of duty or outward expectations will find his work a chore – and his halfheartedness will be communicated. But he who bears witness to "the grace of our Lord Jesus Christ, the love of God and the communion of the Holy Spirit" with glad and grateful heart will find liberty in his testimony and joy in the fruits thereof.

The prime *certainty* of Christian faith and life is that God was – and is – in Christ, through whom "God chose to reconcile the whole universe to himself, making peace through the shedding of his blood upon the cross – to reconcile all things, whether on earth or in heaven, through him alone." (Colossians 1:20) This is our assurance and hope; "this is the gospel to be proclaimed in the whole creation under heaven, and of which we have been made ministers," as Paul and all the saints have been before us. But again, and by the same token, this is also our prime certainty in evangelism. We preach Christ – and ourselves as servants to those for whom Christ died. This is by no means as simple as it sounds – the age-old controversies about Christology are not mere sound and fury. The Christian evangel has all too often been stultified, in proclamation and hearing, by distorted interpretations of Jesus of Nazareth. But the center and core of Christian certitude is here in this mystery – simple in its mystery, personal in its profundity: "Jesus Christ, who of God is made unto us our wisdom and righteousness, and sanctification, and redemption." (1 Corinthians 1: 30) Here we must speak carefully but confidently – of the man of God's own choosing, one of our own humankind, in and through whom we have to do with God himself, no less and none other.

The prime *dynamic* of the Christian life is the vital energy of the Holy Spirit in every human heart, the divine life in Christ's body the church. Many things are useful in the life of the church (organizations, structures, etc., etc.) but only one thing is needful absolutely: the life-giving, life-building, life-crowning operation of the Holy Spirit, who orders the church through his charisms and gifts and who unites the faithful in the sacramental fellowship over which he presides and which he consecrates. But also, and in the same way, the chief dynamic of valid evangelism is the power and prevenience of the Holy Spirit. In all we say and do, we presuppose that the Holy Spirit is already *there*, awakening faith, preparing the heart and mind and will. This does not reduce man's share in the process to insignificance, but it does set up priorities between God's untrammeled freedom and initiative and human responsibility (which is to say, man's ability to respond!).

The prime and constant *end* of the Christian life is the actualization in feeling and act of God's righteous rule in the human community – which is to say, "the kingdom of God." We hear brave talk in various quarters about "bringing in the Kingdom here on earth" – like the Age of Aquarius, whose wistful advent and passing was so brief and pathetic. The Bible never falls into the utopian subjunctive. It says, rather, that God's kingdom is "at hand," that God's reign in righteousness, peace, and joy is a present, live possibility – not by coercion or imposition but by repentance, conversion, obedience. It is the

Christian's foremost task to seek and do God's will as revealed in Christ – and to bring all other goals and values into willing subordination to that will. Only if God's will is norm for our own wills can there be any such thing as a *Christian* ethical decision, or *Christian* wisdom about life.

Once again, I hope the parallel is plain. The chief end of evangelism is that men should hear – really hear – the good news that God's kingdom, God's rule, God's governance is a live option for *them* – in their own "Here" and "Now," oppressed as they are by all the tyrannies of unfreedom, demoralized as they are by the frustrations of freedom abused. The most essential and distinctive connotation of the word "evangelical" is just precisely the primacy of God, of God's kingdom in human hearts, of God's sovereign grace – and of faith as man's radical dependence upon God, before and beyond all other dominions and powers. "Evangelical" does not mean a whole theology or a single denomination: it was a tragedy when "evangelical" came to be an antonym to "catholic." "Evangelical" bespeaks a *dimension* (the *vertical* dimension) of Christian existence – and so also must "evangelism." The essence of sin, as Paul suggests in Romans 1:25, is that in their search for self-governance, men have actually swapped off the *truth* (i.e. that God is sole ruler of all creation) for a lie (i.e. that man is or can be his own savior). As a result, they have come to worship and serve the creature rather than the Creator. The Christian evangel, therefore, is a gracious invitation to turn from our self-maintaining, self-deluding lies to a new and glad reliance upon God as revealed in Jesus: from self-serving devotion to created values, however noble, to a trustful worship of and dependence on the Uncreated Source of all we love and cherish and aspire to.

Finally, the principal *means* in the Christian life for measuring up to God's *expecting* love is God's grace. Wesley was fond of the phrase, "the means of grace" – in his third "General Rule" he used it to include "the public worship of God; the ministry of the Word, either read or expounded; the Supper of the Lord; private prayer; searching the Scriptures, fasting or abstinence" (i.e. intentional self-denial). All of which is meant to point to our spirit's hidden hunger for the sacramental hallowing of all levels and orders of Christian living. The Christian life is sacramental in its inmost depths. Items and events of our lives are made holy and sanctified not by their own quality or any hocus-pocus of ours, but because God chooses to disclose himself and his will for men in and through physical and historical events.

Sacraments are outward and visible signs of God's inward and invisible grace. This means that it is God's Word Incarnate who is the Sacrament that defines all other sacraments but that all of them have this common character: the Word made visible in human history. We can neither possess God's grace nor dispense it by any magic runes or ritual procedures. Instead, we open our hearts to God's present, active personal love (which is what we mean by "grace") and we discover new strength and joy in such an atmosphere. Wesley taught his people to pray: "that we may be enabled by [God's] grace to walk before thee in holiness and righteousness all our days."

In like manner, all valid evangelism must depend on the grace of God, and on the means of grace, or else become distorted. The aim of the evangelist is to call people not merely to repentance and conversion, but also to incorporation, to an engrafting into the body of Christ and to a lifelong process of nurturing and growth in this sacramental fellowship. We call men to Christ, to be sure, but this means incorporation into the church, participation in "the means of grace which [the church] alone supplies." Evangelism is never a private affair: it is the outreaching hand and heart of the *People* of God, drawing men into the fellowship of faith and grace.

But just here we run into a scandalous discrepancy – just as Wesley did – between the evangelical impulse and the ecclesiastical reality. What happens to men who hear the gospel, who confess Jesus Christ as Lord, who join the church and then sink into a spiritual slump under the numbing weight of nominal, formal, perfunctory Christianity? We know very well what happens and it convicts us all of a monumental hypocrisy. In more instances than we can bring ourselves to admit, the local congregation is simply not a healthy setting for a newborn Christian to be initiated into with any lively hope of growing up into Christ, "in holiness and righteousness," etc. Having come to bear the name of Christ as his badge of identity, he often comes to wear it in name only – which is, of course, what "nominal Christianity" means. All of us know this and we are deeply disturbed by it, in varying measure and with varying reactions – most of them one-sided and fueled more by outrage than grace and wisdom.

Let me resort to some vague and imprecise labels to indicate some of these one-sided and ineffectual reactions. The "liberal" Establishment is deeply disturbed and newly defensive but can think of nothing better thus far than redoubled emphases on education, propaganda, and administrative pressures. Most of the curial types I know (in our boards and agencies) still believe that if the right programs (i.e. *their* programs) are pushed hard enough, nominal Christians will somehow be transformed into convincing witnesses for Christ. Then there are the liturgy-and-worship buffs, who seek renewal in the church by means of liturgical innovations and new forms and values in worship, but rarely with a truly catholic sense of sacramental realism and often with a blithe insensitivity to the instincts and tastes of the people at large (who also lack a vivid sense of sacramental realism). The newly self-conscious "evangelicals" are beginning to find themselves and to gird for political contestations with the "liberals," and the "litniks," and "radicals," etc., etc., but still largely within the theological stereotypes of nineteenth century revivalism. The secularizers have a wager going that if the church were only willing to open and empty itself into the world, both church and world would be renewed thereby, as if the church were not already so deeply secularized that the world has written it off as not much more than just another voluntary, cultural association. The revolutionaries have a curiously exaggerated estimate of the resources and influence of the church — as in "the Black Manifesto," "Jonathan's Wake," or "The Sons of Thunder." If the church really wanted to, they trumpet to the world, it could end the war, it could abolish poverty, liberate the blacks, browns and reds, it could usher in Utopia. And they will have it so or else they will try to wreck the system.

All of these polarities have real warrants, but none of them really seems to care or hope for a church that is truly catholic, truly evangelical, and truly reformed, *all together*. None of them, as far as I can see, holds any real promise of transforming the mass of nominal Christians into a vital company of men, women, and youth who truly believe the whole gospel of Jesus, who understand their belief in truly contemporary terms, and who are prepared to act out their faith in life-changing, world-changing social, economic, and political action.

Wesley was quite unwilling to separate evangelism from liturgy, or from the sacramental life of the church, or from social revolution. He stubbornly refused to let his societies secede from the Church of England — even when, as at times, he was almost single-handed in such a refusal — because he knew that evangelism outside a context of the sacramental means of grace is as finally invalid for the converted as are the means of grace for the unconverted. And in the centuries since, as the Methodists have evolved into churches of their own without losing their societal traditions altogether, these polarities between evangelism, Christian nurture, missions, and social action must surely be one of the developments Wesley would least approve.

For he understood, as we had better, that a vital part of the church's evangelistic mission is – *to herself!* Nominal Christians are as obvious postulants for the hearing, and rehearing, of faith, for the excitements and joys of life in the Spirit as any of the unchurched – and until the proclamation of the Christian evangel occurs as the witness of a vital, life-giving church, the Word made audible will not become the Word made visible and it will continue to fail of its full effect.

Give us a church whose members believe and understand the gospel of God's healing love of Christ to hurting men and women. Give us a church that speaks and acts in consonance with its faith – not only to reconcile the world but to turn it upside down! Give us a church of Spirit-filled people in whose fellowship life speaks to life, love to love, and faith and trust respond to God's grace. And we shall have a church whose witness in the world will not fail and whose service to the world will transform it. What can *you* do – what can this Congress, or the Methodist people, do – to help give us such a church?

III: A Third Great Awakening?

n a way, the Wesleyan Revival did not begin in England but in America. On October 11, 1739, John Wesley – walking from London to Oxford – read Jonathan Edwards' newly published *Faithful Narrative of a Surprising Work of God in New England* and was deeply moved by Edwards' vivid account of men and women in paroxysms of anxious guilt finding deliverance and peace in the gospel of God's unmerited grace. This was part of an extensive revival covering almost the whole of the seaboard strip of the young American colonies. Whitefield was involved in it, along with the Tennents, James Davenport, *et al.* It was an evangelism rooted largely in terror. Its converts were men and women whose Protestant independence had left them standing alone before God, without priestly mediation and with a greatly heightened dread of damnation. Edwards' famous sermon, "Sinners in the Hands of an Angry God," was a sort of hyperbolic mirror of the mood in which the gospel was conceived in that age, by sinners and saints alike. Edwards was a great religious psychologist and he had discovered that the gospel was not liable to be heard by these guilt-ridden men and women until they had been deeply shaken with gusts of wild emotion. Then, if ever, the still small voice of God's miraculous mercy might be heard in the heart by faith. Edwards noticed that this sort of "hearing of faith" followed no empirical rules and affected only a few – which lent plausibility to his doctrine of predestination. But the chief characteristic of what came to be called "The First Great Awakening" was a vivid personal experience of deliverance from the wrath to come, and of God's unmerited mercy. "There is a difference," said Edwards, "between having an opinion that God is holy and gracious, and having a sense of that holiness and grace – just as there is a difference between having a rational judgment that honey is sweet and having a sense of its sweetness. . . . The former rests only in the head . . . but the heart is concerned with the latter."

The typical sign of authentic faith, for the evangelicals in this first "Great Awakening," was conversion: a decisive change of heart and mind and will – from guilt to a cleansed conscience, from despair to trust. Given this, the niceties of theological distinctions and church formalities were almost eagerly dispensed with.

Thus it was that the first upwelling of evangelical Christianity in America gave the struggling churches a lively sense of hope and expectation. It provided four-fifths of the Christians in America with a common understanding of the Christian life and faith, and it broke their ties of dependence upon Europe. It supported the notion of "unity in the Spirit," even as it also undercut any idea of organic union. This guaranteed the multiplication of Protestant denominations without let or hindrance. It gave pietism a new and more theatrical style and it settled the previously open question as to whether or not America was to have a powerful indigenous Christianity.

This first Great Awakening ran an uneven course from the 1730's down to the eve of the Revolution. In this last phase, it was joined by Methodists who had migrated from Ireland or who had been sent over by Wesley. They found the American situation different in two crucial ways: (1) here they had no effective church context to provide the catholic sacraments and (2) Wesley's stern disapproval of the Revolution had the effect of canceling his practical authority over the American Methodists.

The Revolution left the churches in a shambles, with greatly reduced numbers and influence (down to five or six percent of the population in 1790). The impact of deism and French Enlightenment thought were strongly ascendant. It was an open question whether orthodox Christianity would survive or wither away in America's new atmosphere of religious liberty and state-church separation. Voltaire and his friends had confidently predicted Christianity's demise wherever freedom came to flourish – and in 1800 the prospects were better than ever that this was what was going to happen in America; just as, later, it did happen, under analogous circumstances, in Australia.

It was the Second Awakening that turned the tide again. You either know its strange and wonderful history or you will not expect me to sum it up in these circumstances. But it was just this immense and complex upwelling of the Spirit that rescued the Christian cause and defined American Protestantism for the better part of a century. It reconquered the Eastern seaboard from the deists; it helped conquer the opening frontiers of the boisterous West. It invented the camp meeting as a new way of getting the gospel to the people. It turned revivalism from an episodic affair to a permanent institution. It relegated the sacraments and Christian nurture to a marginal role and its own theological ethos came to be identified as the distinctive meaning of the word "evangelical" in America. For many – maybe for most – Americans, the word "evangelical" still holds the basic meaning acquired by it in this *Second* Great Awakening. There is no way to understand the anomalies of the modern evangelical movement without re-entering and reassessing this epoch of its greatest success. Only then can we raise the question as to how its good essence might be updated and reborn in this really new world of the late twentieth century – and how much of its archaism might wisely be discarded. There will be no *Third* Great Awakening in America until we come to terms with the fact that the *Second* is over and done with. And yet this is part of what our current confusions are all about.

The most obvious feature of the Second Awakening was its emotional fervor – always focused on two points, and almost only these two: (1) salvation – deliverance from sin and guilt (hellfire and damnation) and (2) a self-inhibitory personal morality. From the first came the outpourings of joy and gladness that resounded in every prayer and testimony meeting; from the latter, the image of the true Christian as one who has forsworn all needless self-indulgence, for whom temperance is total abstinence, whose chastity is prudery and who regards this world as a restless antechamber to the next.

The Second Great Awakening represented the effective triumph in the New World of that "radical Protestantism" that had been so sternly suppressed in Europe by the dominant Lutheran, Reformed and Anglican state-churches. This Protestant tradition was largely "Montanist" in its ecclesiology (low church, free church): anti-sacerdotal, anti-sacramental, anti-intellectualist. It made a pejorative distinction between speculative theology and existential faith. It was suspicious of a learned clergy. It regarded conversion as more typically the climax of Christian experience than its initiation. It insisted on personal religion as the only real essence of Christianity.

And yet the revivalists were also energized in their mission by a rousing vision of a Christian America that would be the natural, though indirect, consequence of a population of converted Christians. Now, almost with nostalgia, Professors Marty of Chicago and Handy of Union Theological Seminary have collected the fascinating evidence that this dream and expectation was the primitive substance of what came to be called "the social gospel." But those of us with a rootage in the evangelical tradition have understood this since childhood. Converted men, we were taught to expect, will convert the economic, social and political order — in some inevitable cause-effect sequence. And this vision of the coaptation of Christianity and American culture inspired the evangelicals to heroic efforts. And it *was* a heroic effort. Not since the Celtic missionaries risked their lives and sanity amidst the Gothonic savages of northern Europe (i.e. the ancestors of these same new Americans) had more zeal, courage, and self-denial been poured into the Christian mission.

The result was a baffling proliferation of denominations and sects — almost one for every contentious evangelist and at least one for every major controversial position. Denominational competition added excitement to the religious scene. For example, the fierce debates between Methodists and Presbyterians about predestination and free will, or those between the Methodists and the Baptists and Campbellites over baptism, were major cultural events in many regions.

It was in this epoch and under these circumstances that what came to be called "evangelical theology" took shape — less by conscious, critical reflection than in response to popular piety. It is very much worth our effort to understand this particular development for it is the fountainhead of what many self-styled evangelicals still regard as orthodoxy, pure and undefiled — hence their fear of and opposition to everything else.

"Evangelical theology" was born in controversy with American deism and this shut it off from the great nineteenth century revolution of thought and feeling that was happening at the same time and that produced the *modern* world. Most of what we know today about science, technology, economics — or about geography, for that matter — stems from the nineteenth century. The nineteenth century marks the profoundest mutation ever experienced in Western civilization up to that time. Almost *none* of this was reflected in the theology of the Second Great Awakening, except by way of negation and rejection. By the same token, however, the revivalist theology had no deep roots in the historic Christian tradition and it developed all sorts of excuses to ignore its larger Christian legacy. Wesley they knew, somewhat, and other eighteenth century pietists – but not much, really, about Luther or Calvin and even less about anything Christian before the Reformation. At the same time, their mistrust of rational*ism* easily passed over into a mistrust of reason itself, except for apologetic purposes.

This shut them up to Scripture and experience as their doctrinal norms and with this they were well-content. But they read Scripture with crassly supernaturalistic hermeneutical principles. The typical revivalist preacher knew more about heaven and hell than Dante or Milton and took it all much more literally. His conception of God was frankly anthropomorphic and his Christology was Eutychian – which is to say, heretical – without his knowing the definition of Eutychianism (i.e. the doctrine that Christ's human nature was absorbed into and dominated by the divine nature). For most of them the virgin birth was taken more as a proof of Christ's divinity than of his humanity. Substitutionary atonement was their only theory of the saving work of Jesus Christ. They spoke often of the Holy Spirit but usually in terms of *personal* charisms rather than of the work of the Spirit in the church and the sacraments. Their anthropology and demonology were Miltonian without Milton's sophistication; their psychology was dualistic or trichotomous; their epistemology precritical, prescientific, and simplistic. In it all, one can recognize the *theologia cordis* of à Kempis, Spener, Francke, and Wesley, uprooted from its original church matrix and lacking any catholic sense of the church and the sacraments.

What the revivalist's reliance really came down to was "Christian experience" and, specifically, the experience of "being saved." The individual believer, in this view, was the sole agent of knowledge, conscience, guilt, and justifying faith; he had no mediator before God save Christ on the Cross and Christ in the heart. His gospel was the assurance of his sins forgiven, his richly merited damnation miraculously averted. *Laissez-faire*, free enterprise, seemed the only conceivable relationship of Christianity and culture. If he was anti-intellectualist – as he was – it was because he believed that the converted heart had all the resources it really needed for requisite decisions in doctrine, ethics, politics, and whatever. If his religion was otherworldly, it was because of his conviction that this world was so obviously no final resting place for man's immortal spirit. If he was sectarian, it was because the truth itself marks out a straight and narrow way. And for many evangelicals, their Christian experience was centered on the one experience that served as a benchmark for all the others: their conversions, with dates, places and autobiographical circumstances forever memorable. Such Christian nurture as they were ever interested in was the replication in some sense or other of this pivotal climax of their Christian lives.

The personal life of the converted Christian was deeply moral. Sobriety, chastity, thrift, industry, decency, and a strict personal integrity were the evangelical's cardinal virtues. But these high personal standards often failed to generate any acute social sensitivity. The heyday of the Revival was also the heyday of the African slave trade and Indian genocide. These were evils deplored and mitigated by some, but not actually prevented or deeply repented of. All the churches were opposed to slavery, but took their impotence in secular, economic and political decisions for granted; abolitionism was viewed by many church leaders as disruptive. Thus it was that the gathering storm of civil war and then the war itself marked the effective end to the Second Great Awakening, just as the Revolutionary War had squelched the First.

The half-century after the Civil War was an epoch of westward expansion and of industrialization – and of the belated impact of European Protestant liberalism on American evangelicals. Horace Bushnell had already proposed his gradualistic formula for Christian nurture as an explicit alternative to revivalism, but his influence was not fully felt until it was reinforced by other powerful liberal tendencies: the impact of science and especially evolution, the rise of historical literary criticism, Schleiermacher's radical shift for the meaning of the term *experience* (from a specific inner sense of God's forgiveness to a much more abstract notion of man's absolute dependence in general), Ritschl's advocacy of social Christianity and, finally, the rise of the so-called "social gospel," from Washington Gladden to Walter Rauschenbusch.

There was an evangelical tendency in liberalism itself nourished by a strong Christocentrism, together with a vivid stress on personal salvation and spiritual life. But in all its variants, liberalism entailed a theology of immanence, of historical and ethical relativism, and of gradualism as the normal pattern of Christian growth and fulfillment. Conversion became the exception rather than the rule, church membership was approved as a substitute for intensive small group experience – and the older patterns of stringent church discipline (probation, doctrinal and moral supervision, heresy trials and excommunication) were slowly eroded and abandoned. Evangelical other-worldliness was more and more translocated in *this* world: man's hopes of God's coming kingdom were focused more and more on the human responsibility to prepare the Kingdom's way. And this led gradually to the most crucial change of all, as far as the Wesleyan tradition is concerned: the displacement of the older optimism of grace (i.e. the expectation of "being made perfect in love in this life") with a new optimism based on moral and spiritual progress. The holiness movement in general had become doctrinaire, simplistic and insufferably self-righteous – at odds with the hierarchy and the generality of laymen as well. The expulsion, or suppression, of the so-called "Holiness Associations" left the Methodists in an ironic plight. One of the basic pillars of the Wesleyan doctrine had been toppled – and it has not yet been restored. Even the modern evangelical is often uneasy with the traces of the doctrine of Christian perfection in our *Discipline, Hymnal* and the other devotional classics – or else he still clings to the distortions of Wesley's doctrine of perfection as they devolved over the course of the nineteenth century in American Methodism.

To some extent, perfectionism was displaced by the soaring hopes of a new humanity in the new age toward which mankind is progressing, inspired and led by Christian faith, nurture, and missionary outreach. John Addington Symond's version of this vision is still in our Hymnal (# 198, *The Methodist Hymnal,* 1964, 1966):

> *These things shall be: a loftier race*
> *Than e'er the world hath known shall rise*
> *With flame of freedom in their souls*
> *And light of knowledge in their eyes.*
> *They shall be gentle, brave, and strong,*
> *To spill no drop of blood, but dare*
> *All that may plant man's lordship firm*
> *On earth and fire and sea and air.*
> *. . . And every life shall be a song,*
> *When all the earth is paradise.*

Talk about perfectionism, *or* millenarianism, *or* utopianism! Incidentally, of course, they all amount to the same thing, psychologically.

For a generation or so (1890-1930+), the newly emergent liberalism was a minority movement, coexisting in uneasy tension and rivalry with the still dominant patterns of evangelical theology. But then, almost suddenly (as historians view the normal rate of change), the evangelicals had lost control and liberalism had become

"Establishment," in the seminaries and then afterwards in the connection generally. It was one of the swiftest and most drastic shifts of theological climate I know of in any tradition. Liberalism's great slogans were focused on the social gospel ("where cross the crowded ways of life" – and this *before* the population explosion!), on Christian education ("the evangelization of the world in *this* generation!"). This is how we got the great ruling empires of the modern Methodist curia – the boards of "missions," "education," and "social concerns."

But culture-Protestantism's soaring optimism was rudely checked by the successive tragedies of the two world wars, the great depression in between, and the rise of totalitarianism: communism, fascism, and nazism. The liberal dream persisted but the dreamers grew more anxious and less certain in the face of repeated disenchantments. This set the stage for a new spasm of transcendentalism that came to be labeled with the clumsy rubric, "neo-orthodoxy": e.g. Barth, Brunner, the brothers Niebuhr, and even Paul Tillich. The common theological project shared by all these "neo-orthodox" theologians was their effort to combine, in one combination or another, nineteenth century liberalism with sixteenth century orthodoxy. It was a great epoch in theology but its direct impact on Methodism was very nearly negligible. Boston personalism, Ritschlian moralism, the social gospel, religious education, global missions – all these were too powerfully entrenched to be shaken much by the fierce critique of culture-Protestantism levied by our neo-orthodox critics.

Meanwhile, a strange alternative to liberalism for evangelicals who wanted to be "modern" had appeared in the guise of "Christian existentialism." I used to puzzle over the easy conversion of fundamentalists and pietists to existentialism in seminary – this was a familiar pattern in the 1950's and early 1960's – until I realized that the axial notions of both views are a vivid faith in "experience" together with a lively mistrust of reason (which is to say that existentialism shares the same psychological character that revivalism did, only with very different rhetoric and a very different lifestyle).

The death-of-God hurrah and the flurry about Christian secularity have had little or no theological substance of their own – an affair of third-rate theologians being taken much too seriously, by themselves and others. But it was a shattering episode all the same: a shocking revelation of what had happened to a Protestantism that had been bred up by two great Evangelical Awakenings, when it had gone for a full century without a *Third* Great Awakening! Along with the radicals and utopians of the new left and the rise and spread of secular mysticisms of all sorts, "the death-of-God" stands as a sort of signal for the end of the Enlightenment, the check of liberal optimism, the emergence of a new breed of modern man. It is as if the program of Feuerbach (that theology must be reduced to anthropology) had finally been accepted four full generations after its original formulation. But more: it threw a depressing light on the swift fading of neo-orthodoxy and existentialism as powerful theological options. When, a few years back, I was asked to survey the contemporary theological scene for an international conference, the metaphor that kept coming to mind was "A View from the Beach at Ebb Tide." And as far as theology is concerned, its current status is still at mean low water. We are still in a time that puts me in mind of that plaintive text in Acts 13:15 – where the rulers of the synagogue in Pisidian Antioch said to Paul and his congregation: "Friends, if you have anything to say to the people by way of encouragement, by all means let us hear it!"

Meanwhile, back to the "evangelical" ranch, things are stirring once again – over and beyond the marginal, guerrilla activities that have been their standard operational procedures ever since the triumph of liberalism. One hears talk nowadays of evangelicals as an organized political power bloc and of their plans for recovered influence in the General Conference and elsewhere – which is fair enough (the liberals certainly understood the ecclesiastical uses of political power). And it may be O.K. – that is, if the process of clamoring pressure groups is to be taken as the ideal agenda for our g-r-e-a-t "ecclesiastical democracy."

But it is just here that my doubts begin to rise and multiply. One of the more probable conclusions from this skimpy historical survey (that could, of course, have been extended cruelly!) is that the theological perspectives and spirit of the Second Great Awakening cannot possibly suffice to stir or guide a Third such upwelling of the Spirit in the last third of the twentieth century – unless they are radically updated and freely transvaluated in truly "modern" terms. And if the cause of evangelism continues to be tied too closely to the resurgent residues of nineteenth century biblicism, supernaturalism, anti-intellectualism, political conservatism, etc., it will simply fail to generate the necessary power and relevance for anything really fresh and new.

What I'm really hoping and praying for, therefore, is not the replication of the Second but the birth of a *Third* "Great Awakening" – a reinvigoration of the evangelical spirit, a revival of God's sovereign grace, a renaissance of the vitalities of the Christian tradition. The first two "Awakenings" saved America from the clear and present dangers of secularism in their times, but these are different times and what sufficed five generations ago will not do so now – save as a rearguard action or a cultural anachronism.

I have tried to explain, in small part and by faint indirection, why any such Third Awakening in American Christianity has been so belated. The first was snuffed out by the Revolution and the challenge of deism. The second was also stultified by war and by the failure of "Christian America" to deal effectively with the horrid consequences of slavery, segregation and with violated human rights in general, *or* with economic and social injustice, *or* with the scourge of war, *or* with the revolution of rising expectations over the earth. The Second Great Awakening was followed by a century of wars, booms-and-busts, disenchantments and forebodings, and yet also a century in which more of mankind have progressed in more ways than in any other century in recorded history. But in this dizzy progress (if that is what it was!) the modern world has "come of age" – in an exhilarating triumph of freedom achieved and a depressing tragedy of freedom abused. Within these new worldviews and in this new intellectual and cultural climate (where religion is largely written off as a major social force), the old traditions simply have to be transvaluated. There is no way for the evangelical syndrome of the *Second* Great Awakening to replicate its effects in this new world.

And yet without its contemporary equivalent in the church in our time, her future and the world's future is bleak indeed. Neo-orthodoxy is already a spent force, partly because of its dependence on those anxiety-guilt feelings that are no longer dominant in the psyches of the young and the radicals, and partly because of its archaic politics (e.g. Barth's condemnation of Nazism and condonation of communism). Liberalism may survive in spirit – the spirit of openness to the risks of freedom – but its cheerful dogmas as to what man can do for himself are increasingly incredible. The hullabaloo about Christian secularity was an important reminder that the Christian mission is in, and to, and for, the world; but once that platitude is granted, what follows? Harvey Cox's progression from *The Secular City* to *The Feast of Fools* is an exercise in trivialization.

Thus, in the winter of our discontent, when the cries of renewal are heard throughout the land, there are no immediately hopeful omens in any of the current movements in the renewal business. None of the crises of war, race, poverty, or ecology is in sight of being solved by the prophets of the new age, or by the trustees of the status quo. The liberal manifestoes of our General Conference do more to salve the consciences of their partisans than to grapple with the problems themselves, or actually to persuade the huge minority of bulldozed dissenters in the church. It is already clear that the New Left has neither the capacity nor the moral character for effective political leadership; but the elections of 1970 also showed that America is not yet ready for any reckless lurch to the right. The young are filled with moral indignation but have been emptied of intellectual curiosity – and even so, their moral indignation would appear to be more herky-jerky than sustained. The cause of human dignity for *all* American minorities – and the female majority as well! – is a holy crusade (all the more so because of its malign neglect by the WASP majority) but even these crusades are faltering, having been badly served by extremism and violence. Renewal is our only hope; but our hopes for renewal can scarcely rest on any of the current renewalist programs I happen to have heard about. Mainstream Protestantism, in the forms we have known it, will not survive this century without a *third* "Great Awakening" of some sort or other!

But of what sort? It must, of course, be evangelical, but, it must, by the same token, be "modern." It will have to come to terms with modern science, especially the developing "sciences of man." It will have to recognize the anthropologized psychologized center of contemporary human self-consciousness; it will have to be "social," "political," this-worldly, etc., etc. In short, the mind-set of the Second Great Awakening (which still seems to some as "the faith once for all delivered to the saints") will have to be transcended. The hearing of faith takes place in the context of the *hearer's* worldview (not that of the preacher's) – and the modern hearer's worldview has been changed out of all recognition over the past century. We could – we even might! – have a powerful resurgence of nineteenth century revivalism, privatism, other-worldliness, but *that* will not be the Third Great Awakening we need, either in scope or impact.

Any truly significant new Awakening must also be deeply concerned about the church, not chiefly in terms of her polity or structure, but as the community of faith and the trustee of the means of grace. And it will have to be ecumenical. The interest of Christians in significant church unity is currently in a slump, but the cause of Christian unity is still the only conceivable base for truly effective

Christian mission and witness. The persistence of sectarian tempers and anti-ecumenical bias amongst some of the self-styled "evangelicals" I know is one of their least attractive features. Evangelism in the next Awakening will surely have to be social-action oriented – and this ought not to seem unprecedented. In its own way, the camp meeting was where part of the social action of that day was "at." Nowadays, the evangelist must also find where the action really is and go there: in patterns and forms of witness and service that may yet have to be invented. And why not? The Great Commission does not say: "Be ready when the world comes knocking at your door," – but rather: "Go ye into all the world," etc.

And above all, the next Great Awakening will surely be pneumatological – an unprogrammed outpouring of the Holy Spirit. One of the clearest signs of the times is the hunger of technological man for the mystical and mysterious, for new explorations into the personal, interpersonal and arcane. It's all being so tragically abused by the countercultures, by psychedelic drugs, by the mantras of bogus Zen, by tarot cards, astrology, and witchcraft. But it's there, it's insatiable, it cries aloud for meaningful expression. And the formalized churches are simply unable to meet this uprising need – just as the "Old Light" preachers were impotent a hundred years ago. It's ironic, isn't it, that this epidemic of mysticism spreads at the very time when the prayer life of nominal Christians is at an all-time low ebb?

It's an old story, though, that the tides of the Spirit are often gathering in out-of-the-way places in just those times when the lights in the temple are flickering low. And every now and then, at least, I think I see some evidence that this is what's beginning to happen now. I can think of the three recent convocations of evangelism that are important milestones – at South Bend and Minneapolis and Dallas – or, indeed, of this one, plus the plans afoot to put evangelism at the heart of the concerns of the World Methodist Council – and the even broader and more ambitious project of Key '73. I recall Ira Gallaway's letter in the last issue of the *Christian Advocate*, with its interesting redefinition of "the modern evangelical" – "one who sees Christian commitment and involvement in all the issues and problems of the world as essential to an authentic expression of Christian faith ..., with a new motivation to be a real agent for change in the world." There are comparable signs of renewal in the lay witness movement in which, for all my misgivings about its crudities and excesses, I recognize a crucial current instance of the Word being made visible as well as audible. My most obvious difficulty with that movement, as I know it, is the fact that many of its typical theological notions are still more archaic than really and truly orthodox, in any classic sense of that much abused but great term.

The signs of spiritual renewal in The United Methodist Church at large are not currently plentiful, as far as I can see. A Methodist General Conference is one of the most spiritually debilitating experiences I ever have, with the last one, at St. Louis, having been the worst. And yet even in this spiritual desert, there are springs and oases: urban churches that are not only still alive but life-giving, suburban parishes that have not fallen victim to the suburban malaise or turned into sensitivity training groups, a few student-work ministries that are serving more than the social action coteries on their campuses, ethnic ministries that are transcending both servility and militancy. In the liturgical movement there is a rising interest in charismatic and relevant worship and an occasional worship-buff interested in sacramental theology as well as in liturgical ballet.

And I must say, albeit with some hesitance and mild embarrassment, that the *most* interesting signs of a new, and just possibly authentic, Third Great Awakening are beginning to be apparent in what strikes me as an unexpected quarter. It is not only that the self-named Pentecostalist groups are gaining in numbers, sophistication and influence in American — and indeed — in world Protantism. What may be even more crucial is the so-called "Charismatic Renewal Movement" in the Roman Catholic Church. The baptism of the Holy Spirit as a conscious experience of conversion, the vigorous renewal of "interior prayer," of small group devotions and mutual nurture, glossolalia and spiritual healing, an evangelical concern for unmediated communion with God through Christ in the Spirit — all this is happening among Catholics in many places in this country and around the world. A friend of mine, Father Kilian McDonnell, O.S.B. (of St. John's Abbey), has been around the world over the past three years, collecting reports and firsthand observations about the development and effects of these groups, and he is convinced that this is the beginning of something epoch-making. Typically, the National Conference of Catholic Bishops doesn't know what to do about it. The bishops can scarcely be expected to endorse it wholeheartedly, but they have also carefully restrained from stifling it. At Notre Dame, it is one of the most vigorous movements on the campus. In the diocese of Dallas, there are several groups of "Spirit-filled persons" that I know of — one of them a group of late teens that strikes me as fantastic. They pray and sing and "rap about Jesus" and then turn up at social action protests. Moreover, they are visibly sane and healthy and are compensating for no neurotic symptoms that I can recognize. One of them was telling me in the most matter-of-fact way how one of his father's friends "got zapped by the Holy Spirit" and had started a little house-church group that now meets every other Tuesday evening. A group of nuns at the University of Dallas who speak in tongues were called up for official assessment – and cleared of canonical impropriety! One of their best theologians was trying to explain to me the other day that this wasn't *his* bag, but that he could not deny the obvious fact of its immense vitality in this movement, together with the evident fruits of love, joy, and peace.

Now, all this frankly baffles me. Pentecostalism is not my bag either – just as it wasn't Wesley's even when people were thrown into hysterical fits by his preaching. But I think I know some of the gifts and fruits of the Spirit when I see them and I am convinced that much of what I have seen is for real – and just may be a portent of something very much more. The Roman Catholic Church is, as we all know, in violent ferment, with all her older authoritarian structures under heavy pressure and some of them in a state of collapse. What an intriguing thought, then, that it just might possibly be these offbeat Catholics – with their evangelical concerns for conversion, with their charismatic baptisms and tongues and with their courageous commitments to reform in both church and society – who just might turn out to be the harbingers of the Third Great Awakening! What if their current charismatic renewal should prove more than a passing fad? Would they be our allies or rivals in our commitments to a church catholic, evangelical, and reformed: catholic in its human outreach, evangelical in its spiritual upreach, reformed in its constant openness to change? If nothing comes of all this, put my comments about it down to a softening of the brain. But if something does come of it, don't say you weren't warned!

A *Third* Great Awakening? It's long overdue, and it cannot possibly be programmed or organized. It is more likely to be led by others beside the professional renewalists; personally I'd shudder to see a Board of Church Renewal set up by the next General Conference. But it's either a third Great Awakening, of whatever sort – or else a further slow decline of the kind of post-Constantinian Christianity that is already passé.

The church stands forever on the rock of faith — assured that the gates of hell will not prevail against her. And we have proof of this over two millennia. But there *have* been long stretches of very nearly suspended animation, in various places and epochs. Such might very well be *our* fate and if so, we'd have no just ground of complaint against Providence. And so, in my daily prayers — along with "Thy Kingdom *come*, thy will be done on earth" — there is often this vision of the church I love in a second spring of the gospel, renewing the hearts of men and the face of the earth, of Spirit-filled men *at peace* and working *for* peace — the glory of God becoming the joy of mankind.

> *Jesus shall reign where'er the sun*
> *Does his successive journeys run,*
> *His kingdom spread from shore to shore,*
> *Till moons shall wax and wane no more.*

If such a vision, tarry, wait for it — and work for it like crazy! But how long, O Lord, how long? Maybe a Congress like this holds a clue to part of the answer to this question!

IV: A Church of Martyrs and Servants

hus far, I have tried to make three main points: (1) that the secret of Wesley's evangelistic success was learning how to make the gospel visible in his own actual social situation; (2) that his evangelical theology has a perennial vitality transcending its eighteenth century worldview and rhetoric; (3) that since the evangelical theology of the Second Great Awakening will not support a *third* without updating and a new synthesis with Christian social action, this project of updating becomes a crucial imperative for us all.

It is in this perspective that I want now to sketch out the dim lineaments of a church I can at least imagine: evangelical, evangelized, evangelistic. I shall be speaking in what I take to be the spirit of the Wesleyan theology, which includes the liberty he felt in translating the perennial gospel of God in Christ into new rhetoric in successive ages.

I have made no bones of my forebodings as to the anguished future of the churches we know in the looming decades ahead. Old epochs do not die, and new ones are not born, without agony and travail. The contemporary church is far too deeply compromised by its century-old acquiescence in nominal Christianity and pattern-maintenance gracefully to absorb the rude shocks of radical change and probable disaster. Our age is credulous of any and all beliefs save the traditional ones and this poses a paradox of over-belief and misbelief. Global peace hangs in the balance of nuclear terror, with ominous detonators ticking away — in Asia, the Middle East, Latin America. Our ecological time-clock is racing out of control; man has become his own worst pollutant. The revolution of rising expectations has raised a myriad of hopes and satisfied none. The countercultures have proved

capable of disruption but not of creativity and continuity. Over the
globe there is everywhere an appalling void of outstanding leadership
– in politics, in the church, in philosophy, art, or whatever. Parkinson's
first "Law" and "the Peter Principle" are working overtime. Where is
there a single statesman, or cleric, or sage, or great artist (in *any* medi-
um) who looms above the generality to lift an ensign for our flagging
hopes? We are immersed in instant communication, most of it ten-
dentious and untrustworthy, which makes for an endemic cynicism
about all communication. The world is a gaggle of true believers hopelessly disagreed as to what is true.

We know all this and yet we have been strangely loathe to recognize the riven chasm it has opened between us and our ancestors and
their traditions. "Human nature never changes," we keep saying, as if
that were a comfort. "All these new developments are variations on
ancient themes" – and of course there is a solid core of truth in this
instinctive appeal to human continuity. But it is also misleading, for it
blurs our perceptions of radical change in the new situation and it
prompts miscalculations of the futures that are being born out of this
new present. This, incidentally, is why the self-styled "theologies of
hope" have struck such a responsive chord in so many bewildered
hearts and yet have shed so little light – and why, again, the avowed
"theologies of politics" promise so much and have achieved so little.

Evangelism's secret of success has always lain in its vivid awareness
of the actual sense of human existence in the current age, whenever
that was, in its ability to translate the eternal verities of the perennial
gospel into new idioms for new generations.

> *To serve the present age, Our calling to fulfill . . . !*

We have, therefore, a good precedent for any effort to reassess the
current scene, again and again, always probing, searching for the
human actuality and what God is doing in it by way of self-disclosure
in Christ through the Spirit. What is God's good news to man's bad
news in this *new* human context, whatever "this new human context"
may be?

The new world I see about us and ahead of us has been shaped, in
part, by three immense and unprecedented developments in human
history – each of them a reversal of an immemorial state of affairs, and
all three of them interactive and interdependent. The first is the triumph of technology – and the fantastic acceleration of change in the
physical circumstances of human existence with all its attendant cul-

tural consequences. This is a phenomenon much better understood by men like Zbigniew Brzenzski and Alvin Toffler than any theologian or preacher I know. This technological revolution and its psycho-socio-logical effects have weakened all our former premises about social stability and have heightened our false confidence of being able to achieve any human goal we can define or aspire to. Our new over-confidence takes the form of a projection: "Any nation that can put a man on the moon, can . . . (you name it)." The effects of this on *self-confidence* – by supplying self-evident "good reasons," for any sort of rude impatience with any status quo! – are incalculable, but their import for evangelism is clear. We are still speaking as desperate men to desperate men, but their own existential definitions of despair are radically different from those that John Wesley and Peter Cartwright could take for granted in their respective epochs.

A second emergent marking off this new epoch is the immense triumph of radical freedom, relative and real. Social control systems, more or less effective for five millennia, are now being transcended – everywhere in principle and almost everywhere in fact. This triumph of freedom has given modern man a bewildering range of over-choice – things to buy, things to do, ways to be – and with this has come a new autonomy, a new antinomianism, a new a-moralism with literally unprecedented social effects. More people – including the very young and even "the wretched of the earth" – have more daily choices that they can make than any generation that ever lived on this planet heretofore. Personal and interpersonal relations are voluntary as never before; the decisive inhibitions of social mores, and of moral and religious taboo have faded, amongst the young especially. The man who knows himself unliberated – for whatever cause – also knows that he *is* free in principle and ought to be in fact. This begets both hope and outrage – what the radicals speak of as "the consciousness of being oppressed." No generation ever understood themselves quite like this before and it makes a radical difference in how they can hear the gospel of "*Christian* liberty."

A third emergent differentiation of our age from its predecessors might be called the triumph of humane values. It is not, of course, a humane age in fact, but it *is* the first one in which human values have been so widely affirmed as paramount. From time immemorial, *some* men have been valued as instrumental to the values of *other* men – and this of necessity. This is what slavery and war and caste-and-class systems, etc., have always been all about. This is the age-old meaning of rank-and-status; the moral essence of kingship and hierarchy and official authority (i.e. the right to decide who is rightly subordinate to whom in what respects). All this is changing radically in theory and rapidly in practice, in all of Western culture and all its cultural spinoffs. Kant's great maxim – that we should treat humanity, whether in ourselves or in others, always as an end and never as a means only – now appears more obvious to more people than ever before. Its frequent denials *in practice* are rarely defended *in principle* – as they used to be. A whole new value scale is emerging around the humane principle itself. And the challenge of this to any traditional theological denigration of the *humanum* goes deeper than some of us have reckoned.

Would he devote his sacred head For such a worm as I?

was once a searching, proper question; it is still so to me. What we must understand, however, is that it is no longer arresting, or even edifying, to the generality of the young.

We live, therefore, in a time of unparalleled victories for the human spirit – technological dominance in and over nature, freedom past the dreams of Jean Jacques Rousseau, the consecration of the *humanum*. All of these are *great* triumphs – and yet also all of them finally hollow – and this is both the grandeur and misery of this new age.

Each one of these great victories of the human spirit has displaced an older, constricted view of the human lot in this world that once seemed utterly natural to our forefathers. The triumph of technology displaces an economy of scarcity with one of affluence. And even if its benefits are largely confined to a fraction of mankind, there are not many actually prepared to abandon the technological order outright – not even its alienated dispraisers. The triumph of freedom has displaced an ethic of conformity with an ethic of choice, actually of over-choice. The structures of arbitrary authority are being displaced by processes of consultation and persuasion (as in the new business procedures of "management by objective"). This triumph of humane values is by way of canceling the assumption that *some* men, under *some* circumstances, can be regarded as means only (instrumental or statistical values) and not as ends in themselves – at least not here and now. These are all great gains – and if the disorders attendant upon their realization offend us to the point of our denying their positive significance, we may fail to recognize how, through even these disorders, God is pointing the way ahead.

As of now, however, they are all hollow victories because they have also exposed so starkly the radical incontinence of the human spirit, our radical finitude, our radical pathos and tragedy. Subhuman animal appetites, as we know, are held in a rough-and-ready ecological equilibrium, by instinct and herd mores. But our truly human aspirations (for knowledge, freedom, love, etc.) are literally insatiable. Nothing in human nature guarantees that men will "naturally" prefer truth over lies, order over disruption, the common good over self-interest. The hope and expectation that this is what would happen, somehow automatically, was the root-fallacy of liberalism. Unless our freedom is normed by order and our love is normed by community, men are newly doomed to neon-lighted hells of their own making here on earth.

The new economies of affluence are already beginning to threaten the human future on this planet. And for all its wonderworking, technology has not yet found a way to narrowing the affluence gap between the developed and the underdeveloped countries – and neither have our economists or statesmen – and if I may say so in all respect, none of the experiments of any of the welfare states nor any of the advertised panaceas of world government hold any lively hope for the human future. I have only to remember what has happened to my beloved Sweden to think that the moral of the Garden of Eden story was actually understated.

The triumphs of freedom have plunged us into the perils of over-choice and of the intolerable pathos of freedom abuses. Ancient sexual taboos have been discarded but the true meaning of conjugal love still goes undiscovered. Drugs and other experiments in self-manipulation are permitted – or at least cannot be inhibited – and yet authentic self-understanding and self-control still elude us. They keep telling us that marijuana is not physically addictive, but not how it dampens psychic motivations and so weakens the fibers of moral character and self-possession. An impressive commission reports no positive correlation between pornography and sex crimes but fails to consider how regularly and inevitably pornography cynically corrupts the essential correlation between human *sexuality* and human *dignity*. Our own General Conference approves cheap and easy abortion (feticide!) in the same session in which it condemns many other modes of human disregard for the sanctity of human life.

The triumphs of freedom have multiplied enchantments and disenchantments. Alvin Toffler points to the proliferation of cults, subcults and countercultures in modern society – all in fascinating diversity but with swift evanescence. But what are the net gains of all of this for the human cause itself? It used to be an article of faith with the liberals that liberated men will govern themselves humanely. This is still an article of *faith*, but it is increasingly incredible.

Or yet again, the consecration of the *humanum* amounts to a bold defiance of Thomas Malthus – and one might cheer for *that*, if only we could find some *other* way to control the runaway growth of the earth's population or some other eugenic program for the biological upgrading of the human species. Our fierce self-confidence that man really does have direction of his earthly career within his jurisdiction and power has brought us, sooner than we expected, to rude disenchantment. Daniel Jenkins, as some of you know, is Director of the Humanum Studies for the World Council of Churches. He is an exceedingly able man, with all the traditional social action biases. But just recently, he let his back hair down with an uncommonly candid blast of *ad interim* pessimism:

> *I do not think one can be blamed for concluding from [our Commission's studies thus far] that by far the most probably true recording of the [present human] situation is that not only is prediction an illusion, but so is planning and so is control . . . . In other words, the situation is getting steadily and rapidly worse while we do not even know how to think about it or talk about it adequately, let alone cope with it.*

This is exactly how I feel when Mr. Nixon tries to reassure us about how well we are coping with the international situation or the national economy.

But we shall miss the point about evangelism in a new world if we conclude from modern man's chantments that he is a fit candidate for regression, back to nineteenth century slogans and inscapes: "Back to the Bible" – and its eighteenth century exegesis; "back to the old-time religion" – i.e. the Second Great Awakening, etc. I know, of course, that there are, maybe, millions of our contemporary ancestors still alive, who can and will hear the gospel in eighteenth century terms and I mean no disparagement of them whatever – and no easement of our obligations to minister to them, in *their* cultural mind-set, according to their spiritual needs. Indeed, I sometimes suspect that they may have to serve as seed corn for survival *after* catastrophe, if it comes to that.

But the modern world is "where it's at," right now and for the foreseeable future that we are responsible for. Our account of the perennial *evangelion* must be addressed to these new dimensions of human self-consciousness – if modern men are to be evangelized. I say this in full awareness of my zealous advocacy of John Wesley as a prime, and still vital, resource for our modern concerns in evangelism, for I am equally eager to make the point that it is Wesley himself who stands as paradigm for me in this business of doing theology for the actual people who are out there to *hear* the gospel – rather than as some sort of inherited template of truth to be pressed down on the hearer's mind, regardless of his own perceptions. Pure doctrine as an end in itself was Wesley's way in the barren years: he learned better after Aldersgate and Bristol.

But even if a rich and complex theology (like Luther's or Wesley's) cannot simply be reduplicated in a later age without appropriate changes and development, how much less hopeful is the stubborn effort to maintain a theological ideology and rhetoric that was already simplistic to begin with and impoverished in its awareness of the total Christian tradition over the centuries. And this, as I suggested last night, was and still is the case with much of the nineteenth century mentality and its survivals. Consider, for example, the so-called "Computer Survey" conducted at the Dallas Convocation last summer – as reported in the current issue of *Good News.* "The survey contained a number of questions planned to gauge doctrinal orientation" – and, presumably, to provide some differentiation between "evangelical" and "liberal" theological categories. The kindest thing one can say of most of the questions as they were reported is that they are baffling – in terms of any sophisticated theological assessment I can imagine. Ninety-three and three-tenths percent were reported to have affirmed the proposition that "Jesus Christ is God." Now, what are we to make of the fact that that statement *in that form* is palpably heretical, since in Scripture and the creeds the *vere Deus* ("truly God") is *always* balanced by the *vere homo* ("truly man") and the further fact that the isolation of the divine from the human nature in Christ is expressly forbidden by the Definition of Chalcedon – i.e. the traditional norm for Christological *orthodoxy*? Is it really the case that 93.3 percent of evangelicals are still self-consciously *monophysite*? If so, then what are we to say about their orthodoxy, biblical and classical? And what are we to make of fundamentalists who have fallen into heresy? It is no excuse to retort that liberals have exalted Jesus' human nature over the divine. Biblical, orthodox Christianity has yoked them both together, without confusion or separation – and anything less than this is something other than "the whole story of Jesus."

Or, again, 55.4 percent are said to have denied that "the Bible has *any* errors or mistakes whatsoever" – and 67.8 percent affirmed that "Jesus will return to earth to preside over a millennial kingdom," otherwise unspecified. Here is an 1820 mind-set yoked to a 1970 computer. And the whole business raises some very serious problems as to whether there is a valid basis for identifying this sort of "evangelical theology," defined in *these* archaic terms, with evangelism as Wesley understood and practiced it.

What is needed, and what may be possible, is a reassessment of the current problems and tasks of traditioning the perennial truths of the eternal gospel, through the vicissitudes of cultural change. The genius of Christian evangelism, over the ages and around the world, has been its flexibility, its power to adapt its message and methods to emerging mindsets, without compromising the vital core and without needless emphasis on time-bound theological opinions. This requires a careful and yet critical familiarity with the whole Bible (but as a speaking book, not as an unsystematic collage of systematic theology). It demands a critical and yet sympathetic acquaintance with the entire Christian tradition – for there is the laboratory where the differences between the core and the fringes of doctrine have been hammered out with greater stability and precision than some of us may realize. And it also means a wholesome and yet wholly unintimidated respect for the mindsets of our own time and for the people who hold them – since *this* is "the field white unto the harvest," into which our Lord is sending us, *now*.

As I see it, the most basic problem in the reformulation of our evangelistic message is the radical dissolution in the modern mind-set of the age-old linkage between anxiety and guilt, between customary and Christian morality, between the wrath of God and social disapproval, between self-loathing and repentance and justifying faith. Always before the classic text for this was Romans 7 – the inner conflict between sin and the Law that could force the desperate query: "Who shall deliver me from this helpless dominion of sin that gains its strength from the Law?" The evidence piles up that *this* "strength of the Law" is no longer the ground-tone of modern anxiety. A vivid sense of guilt *before God* – or fear of hellfire or *any* moral absolute – is increasingly rare. For good or ill, and for reasons that are still obscure, the new antinomianism amongst the young has altered the terms in which human despair is felt and registered. A sign of this is the new pervasive *self*-righteousness one meets in response to *any* sort of social disapproval (especially from the elders of the tribe) and the very nearly universal sense of victimization that makes villains of others – the oppressors! – but that rarely assesses or accepts guilt as one's own unbearable burden before God.

We have scarcely realized the magnitude of this mutation. It marks the end of the dominance of the gospel addressed primarily to self-conscious guilt (the *forte* of fundamentalism) and yet also an end to the gospel of a pure-hearted moral ethic as taught and exemplified by Jesus (the *forte* of liberalism). It means that our 400-year-long assault on moralism, legalism, and the terrors of conscience has succeeded with quite untoward results. Do you know Sammie Smith's currently popular ballad, "Help Me Make It Through the Night" – with its defiant hedonism, its self-conscious a-moralism? "I don't *care* what's right or wrong, etc.!" This is only one of a hundred echoes in contemporary culture of this new moral (or a-moral) consciousness among a widening population in this new age. Luther's terrors and Calvin's thunders leave these people unmoved or incredulous.

What is newly at stake, therefore, is whether the gospel can speak of God's gracious initiative on man's behalf in *whatever* new predicament he may be in, or if it was only the story of what God *once* did for men in the predicaments they were in then. If Jesus Christ is indeed the same – yesterday, today and forever! – then what he means for us men and our salvation, how he stands as our clue to the heart of God and equally our clue as to how we may pass from being barely human to being truly human (before God and in his grace!), then all this must be communicated to the currently unbelieving multitude – and at the same time to the dwindling band of nominal Christians who bear his name but do not share his joy and victory!

This will be no new gospel. Its chief locus will still be in Scripture, its true center is Jesus Christ, and its true vitalities have been manifest throughout Christian history by the threefold action signs of (1) heralding, (2) martyrdom and (3) servanthood – all in Christ's name and spirit, none by itself alone. There is in the New Testament a special trio of dominical imperatives to evangelism that the church has remembered and cherished – and that are still imperative:

1. From the added ending to Mark, "Go therefore into all the world and preach (herald) the gospel to every creature" (Mark

16: 15).

2. From the future-imperative in Acts 1:8, "You shall (must) be my martyrs — in Jerusalem and in all Judea and away to the ends of the earth." The word "martyr" here means, of course, "to bear witness," but not just by words alone — by words embodied in lives that can, if need be, be verified in heroic death. A Christian martyr is a person who puts his life where his mouth is, "in Jesus name"!

3. The third sacrament in John 13, where Jesus gave the disciples their *new* commandment — to love one another as he had loved them — and then had showed them what love really means — i.e. servanthood. "If I, your Lord and Master, have washed your feet, you also ought to wash one another's feet. I have set you an example; you are to do as I have done for you."

There is no doubt at all that Christianity has survived and been sustained through the centuries by a quality of life most visible to others in *martyrdom* and *service*. This was so in the times of persecution: "the blood of the martyrs is the seed of the church." It has also been true in the classic tales of the great conversions: Augustine's, Wesley's, and almost anybody else's you can name. In each case, it was the sight of Christian lives in martyrdom, and service to others, that prepared the way for the Spirit's converting action. In all the great epochs of missionary outreach, it was the church of the martyrs of Christ and the servants of man that actually communicated the gospel. This is why conversions gained by the Cross used as bludgeon or gimmick have rarely served the causes of evangelism *or* Christian nurture *or* missions *or* social action.

The Word must become audible, yes; but, more crucially, it must become visible, exemplary, winsome (literally!). And it is most winsome in the lives of men who have been led by it into joyous and unservile servanthood: men under obedience, men of undaunted courage and unvanquished hope — always in God through Christ in the Spirit. Evangelism is not just Christian truth proclaimed and defended. It is the apostolic benediction acted out: "the grace of our Lord Jesus Christ [in gracious living in the daily round], the love of God [in loving deeds motivated by gratitude to God] and the communion of the Holy Spirit [manifest in a community of those conscious of being members one of another in Christ's body, the church]." Understood in this light, the benediction is no liturgical holding action to give everybody a fair start in fleeing a church at the end of a service. It is, rather, the congregation's marching orders as they fare forth into the world!

But the most distinctive dimension of Christian martyrdom, the least readily suspected of self-interest, was summed up in the Christian concept of service and servanthood. "We do not preach ourselves," said Paul: "we preach Christ, and offer ourselves as your servants for Jesus' sake." Look up the references to "servants" and "servanthood" in the New Testament and then ponder the shocking realization that *doulos* means either "a slave" or at the very least a menial servant. Then try to understand, if you can, what Christian "service" means to free men and proud. Three things at least: (1) that Christ's *slaves* share his liberation by the same almighty power that raised him from the dead; (2) that Christian freedom is a very special form of commitment (rather than release from commitment); (3) that there is *no* human indignity in any act or mode of service that mirrors *God's* love. Nietzsche was right: Christianity is a "slave morality." But he also missed the point: it is the unservile and voluntary self-denial of free men, who have it on the gospel's authority that love is the only real power that does not corrupt the man who receives it, the only power that truly is eternal.

Christian servanthood is the ungrudging offering of God's gifts — of life, talent, resources, whatever — as one's own gifts to others. And this is the hardest part of the gospel to believe and practice. It threatens our two most vulnerable spots: fear of destitution and fear of indignity. These are aboriginal fears and they cannot be allayed in *any* society that cherishes rank and status. We speak too glibly, therefore, of the servant-church and of Christian service, when the fact is that we have confused *benevolence* with *servanthood*. Is this why the church rejected the sacrament of servanthood in John 13, with its unequivocal: "*Do this* — as a sign of your discipleship"? In her struggle to survive in the world, she has taken on the pomps and blazonry of a feudal pecking order, muttering betimes about "the servant of the servants of God." And even yet, when we talk about service, we are all too often involved in anxious bids for power and status and money — as in the familiar euphemism about "a larger field of service."

One thing we have learned from Wesley, or could have, is that evangelism for him was a lifelong martyrdom, an ungrudging outpouring of self in service, in Christ's name and spirit. But one of the words that has never crossed my mind in connection with John Wesley, ever, is "servility." He was as proud as Lucifer! And so, his servanthood in Christ was something else again: the freedom to give himself away in meaningful, useful work and the grace-full love to do this without stint or cunning. It was *this* visible martyrdom and servanthood that rammed home the *evangelion* he preached. He taught his Methodists to be martyrs and servants – in just precisely those terms. They learned it from him and so became evangelists themselves, not many of them as preachers, but all of them as witnesses whose lives backed up their professions.

The world hears the gospel when it sees it – when its witnesses are clearly concerned with human existence and clearly committed to a more fully human future, in this world and the next. It is as corny as Christmas to say so, but truth is that the finally persuasive "martyrdom" (witness) to God's love in Christ and to Christ's love for the last and the least and the lost is a Christ-like life – faith working by love to serve God's righteous rule and to give men hope, *in God*.

Part of what this means in our new future is that our message and witness must take into full account the changed character of human existence, of the changed terms and conditions of the human tragedy. To the starving, we must help them find bread! For the well-to-do, we must help them find a way out of affluence's cruel traps. To the oppressed, we must help them to be free; to the victims of freedom, we must help them find moral commitments that are anchored in God and have some promise of staying power. One of the most pathetic and dangerous aspects of our current moral chaos is the steady erosion of moral commitments. Alvin Toffler has commented on this in *Future Shock*:

> *Value turnover is now faster than ever before in history . . . [and] for the foreseeable future, we must anticipate still more rapid value changes. . . . This is no small and easy matter. It accounts for the much lamented "loss of commitment." . . . [People shift from fad to fad, from style to style but without real rootage in any.] . . . And this forces the problem of over-choice to a qualitatively new level. It forces us to choices not merely among lifestyle components but among whole lifestyles.*

Just here, the Christian lifestyle itself – if unencumbered with externals that once identified it without being essential to it – becomes a live and hopeful *evangelion* to men in their turmoils of bewilderment and panic. The old linkage between anxiety-guilt-legalism, repentance-pardon-salvation from hellfire in a punitive society can now be reforged, without treason, into a message of God's offer of meaning to men in search of meaning, of God's commitments to men who have found nothing to commit themselves to fully, God's stubborn rejection of any final triumphs for *self*-indulgence, *self*-righteousness, *self*-centeredness. Now as never before we need to stress God's offer in Christ to men who are willing to trust his love (i.e. faith), God's gift of hope to men who are eager for a more humanly hopeful future.

For the gospel offers men a choice – in this age of over-choice – the only choice that does not stultify or abuse the freedom exercised in making this choice: the choice of God's sovereign grace in Christ as the sustenance of our life, here and hereafter, the choice of Jesus Christ as Lord and Savior (whose love and service is freedom and joy), the choice of love (to God and neighbor) as life's real and eternal meaning (in weal and woe, in life and death!), the choice of a Spirit-filled life of joy and gentleness and self-control. No such lifestyle as this is available to men as a human achievement. It is a gift – the gift of God's grace; it is accepted by faith and faith alone. Life's highest, deepest meaning is given us by God in Christ, in foretaste and hope that it can and will be lived out, in turmoil and terror and yet also in courage and serenity.

Does this sound less evangelical than Wesley? I hope not – I believe not. The psychological center of his gospel preaching was forgiveness of sins *within the then current scheme of moralistic sin-guilt-and-damnation.* Yet, every stroke of deliverance from the Law was also a hammer blow for a new morality: a synergistic morality that put and kept God the Father *foremost,* Christ the Son *utmost,* and the Holy Spirit *inmost.* Wesley was as vitally concerned as ever the humanists were about the quality and dignity of human life – only he knew, as they did not, that life's highest quality and dignity cannot be *gained,* but must be *given,* that life's enduring meanings and values are all dividends of grace. And in a world where the quality and dignity of human life are still in hazard, the Wesleyan vision of a church of martyrs and servants holds the only hope I see, in the shambles just ahead and for the glory road beyond.

Let me try to illustrate this in closing. Just under two centuries ago, Wesley was laying the foundation of the New Chapel near City Road in London – now a familiar Methodist landmark. It was a conscious act of giving a permanent symbol to a movement hitherto characterized by great mobility ("itinerancy") and adaptability. As he looked back over the amazing four decades that had gone before and then, as he looked down "the future's broadening way," he wanted above all to define the radical essence of evangelical religion so that his people and his successors would understand what was forever *crucial*, and what should always be kept open for theological negotiation and development. He thought he knew the secret of the Revival, and he wanted them to realize what was most essential for its future. And so he summed it all up in a final paragraph that a technical theologian might find dangerously oversimplified. But this must have been *deliberate*, for Wesley was not simple-minded and was at least as sensitive to the clamorous options of theological controversy as we. And so I am convinced that what he said then he would still stand by and would have us do so even now. It does, however, leave open the question as to what would happen to *us* if we took something like *this* as lodestone for our own evangelical theology, as we seek to be a church of the martyrs of Christ and the servants of *his* brethren:

> *[Are you] witnesses [i.e. martyrs] of the religion above described? Are you really such? Judge not one another; but every man look into his own bosom. How stands the matter in your own breast? Examine your conscience before God. Are you an happy partaker of this scriptural, this truly primitive, religion? Are you a witness of the religion of love? Are you a lover of God and all mankind? Does your heart glow with gratitude to the Giver of every good and perfect gift, the Father of the spirits of all flesh, who giveth you life, and breath, and all things; who hath given you his Son, his only Son, that you "might not perish, but have everlasting life"? Is your soul warm with benevolence to all mankind? Do you long to have all men virtuous and happy? And does the constant tenor of your life and conversation bear witness of this? Do you "love not in word" only, "but in deed and in truth"? Do you persevere in the "work of faith, and the labour of love"? Do you "walk in love, as Christ also loved us, and gave himself for us"? Do you, as you have time, "do good unto all men"; and in as high a degree as you are able? Whosoever thus "doeth the will of my Father which is in heaven, the same is my brother, and sister, and mother." Whosoever thou art, whose heart is herein as my heart, give me thine hand! Come, and let us magnify the Lord together, and labour to promote his kingdom upon earth! Let us join hearts and hands in this blessed work, in striving to bring glory to God in the highest, by establishing peace and*

goodwill among men, to the uttermost of our power! First, let our hearts be joined herein; let us unite our wishes and prayers; let our whole soul pant after a general revival of pure religion and undefiled, the restoration of the image of God, pure love, in every child of man! Then let us endeavor to promote, in our several stations, this scriptural, primitive religion; let us, with all diligence, diffuse the religion of love among all we have any intercourse with; let us provoke all men, not to enmity and contention, but to love and to good works; always remembering those deep words (God engrave them on all our hearts!), "God is love; and he that dwelleth in love dwelleth in God, and God in him!"

The lectures contained herein are based on the Fondren Lectures of 1974.

Library of Congress Catalog Card Number: 74-24509

Theology
in the Wesleyan Tradition

I: "Plundering the Egyptians"

our years ago, I tried my hand at translating my research-
es in Wesley into an updated interpretation of *Evangelism
in the Wesleyan Spirit.*[1] That, by definition, was only a partial view of the man and his work (albeit at the beating
heart of it all). Now, I'm concerned to enlarge our angle of vision
somewhat and to propose another interpretive sketch of Wesley this
time *as a significant theologian* whose importance as theologian—then
and now—has been sadly underestimated by both his devotees and
critics. He was, I have come to believe, the most important Anglican
theologian in his century. He is, I also believe, a very considerable
resource in our own time for *our* theological reflections, especially for
those who have any serious interest in the ecumenical dialogue and in
the cause of Christian unity. My aim and hope is to help rescue Wesley
from his status as cult-hero to the Methodists (by whom he has been
revered but not carefully studied) and to exhibit him as a creative
Christian thinker with a special word for *these* parlous times and for us,
as we try to grapple with the new problems created by the current
crises in culture—problems posed by the passing of all the old polarities (Protestant-Catholic-"Enlightenment," etc.) that served to define
so many of our received traditions, now eroded or eroding. For better
or for worse, we are at the end of that cultural syndrome once defined
by: (1) the Renaissance-Enlightenment concern for form and reason;
(2) the Protestant Reformation's insistence upon *sola fide*; (3) the
Roman Counter Reformation's alternative of an authoritarian
church-culture; (4) the mores of a deferential society that supported
patterns and codes of *ex officio* authority; (5) the dominance of
European-North American culture; (6) soaring faith in science and

technology; and (7) the idea of human progress. It is, therefore, a baffling time, a difficult time in which to proclaim the good news of God in Christ as credible and relevant. And yet—although our circumstances are radically different from Wesley's—it is just exactly the sort of crisis that he would have tried heroically to comprehend, confident that the perennial gospel still offers to us in the twentieth century the same eternal truth and hope he himself had proved it had for eighteenth century Englishmen: not only the lively hope of *heaven*, but also a credible hope for a meaningful life in *this* age (and any age) whatever its crises between theology and culture. At any rate, this is my agenda in the following chapters.

Wesley the evangelist is, of course, a familiar figure (actually a stereotype), and so also Wesley the organizer, and even Wesley the social reformer who helped shape a reformation of morals and manners in British life.[2] But what has gone largely obscured is *Wesley the theologian*—specifically, a theologian of culture and, even more specifically, a *folk-theologian* who found effective ways to communicate the gospel to mass audiences who cared little about the complexity of his sources or the cultural import of his evangelistic messages.

Where we must begin, therefore, is with Wesley's eclectic heritage and lifestyle, as a man and as a theologian. He was born into a home where piety and culture had long been blended as a matter of course. He learned to read early and he continued to read and study incessantly throughout a long and busy life. His tastes ranged over the entire literary spectrum, from the classics to what were, in his day, the newest essays, novels, plays, and treatises. It was no accident that he was a favored friend of Dr. Johnson's (the literary panjandrum of Augustan England).[3] He was, moreover, equally concerned with political history and current social change.[4] His life span coincided in a remarkable way with a period in British history that turned out to be its prelude to modernity— so that almost without knowing it, Wesley faced both ways in a bewildering ambivalence (toward the European past that he understood so well and toward the global future that he glimpsed with remarkable prescience). It was, as we know, a great age in the history of science, and Wesley was keenly interested in this—"the latest scientific discoveries," and all that—confident that every advance into scientific truth would reveal "the wisdom of God in creation"[5] to the eyes of faith.

All of which is intended to remind us that Wesley, like most Christian thinkers before him (back to St. Paul), had to grapple with the problem of what we have come to call "secularism": viz., how are the treasures of human culture to be related to and appropriated by a credible Christian theology that appreciates humane wisdom wherever found—without forfeiting its own integrity? Wesley's eclecticism had an honorable history, with great trailblazers before him, whom he knew. There was Origen, the very first Christian theologian with a first-rate classical education. In Exodus 12:18-36 there is that strange story about the departing Israelites applying to their erstwhile Egyptian masters for "gifts." Moreover, says the Exodus historian, "the Lord made the Egyptians well-disposed toward the Israelites and let them have whatever they asked. In this way, they [the Israelites] plundered the Egyptians." A man as sensitive to biblical morality as Origen was bound to feel queasy with such a story (it does sound a bit like ripping off, doesn't it?). And so he came up with an imaginative allegory. "Plundering the Egyptians," he explained, is a *metaphor*, pointing to the freedom that Christians have (by divine allowance) to explore, appraise, and appropriate all the insights and resources of any and all secular culture. Later, St. Augustine, in his *De Doctrina Christiana* would borrow this metaphor as *his* warrant for Christian transvaluations of classical culture.[6] The thoughtful Christian who understands the live core of the gospel and who is deep-rooted in the biblical witness to God's self-revelation is thereby entitled and encouraged to exploit the full range of secular literature, science, and philosophy—always with a view to the enrichment of one's Christian wisdom and the enhancement of his effectiveness in communicating the Christian message. The richer one's "Egyptian plunder" (i.e., one's secular culture) the richer one's understanding of God's wisdom and power in Christ—who, as Logos and Light, is the true illumination for all seekers after truth and wisdom.[7]

This is one of the best of our Christian traditions—evangelical Christians reaching out to discern and evaluate secular wisdoms of every sort. And this is why any theology that is content to be exclusively biblic*ist*, or traditional*ist*, is invalid and finally fruitless—just as, on the other side, any theology without an evangelical focus will soon drown in its surrounding secular milieu. And when you stop to think how much of Christian thought and teaching nowadays tends toward simplistic biblic*ism*, over on the right wing, and Pelagian secular*ism*, on the left (or, sometimes, professedly "traditional*ist*" but with only a shallow, thin "tradition"), one wonders if any further explanation is required for the all too obvious cultural impoverishment of so many of our pulpits and pews.

And just as Wesley understood and practiced this art of "plundering the Egyptians"—their arts and letters, their philosophy and science,
their political and moral insights—so also he challenges us to go and do
likewise. But we had better take careful note as to how skillfully he
managed it—so that his immense erudition never obscured his "plain
words for those plain people" who were his primary audiences by his
own choice. He was one of the few truly successful popularizers in the
history of preaching who never beguiled his audiences and who rarely
oversimplified real issues. His preaching and teaching offered both the
gospel *and* a liberal education, as an integrated experience, to the common people who heard him gladly. What a tragedy, then, that this art of
"plundering the Egyptians" (without remaining in Egypt!) has been so
sadly neglected in our time: so that now we have evangelicals with very
little humane culture to speak of, on one side, and, over on the other,
liberals and secularizers with no deep rootage in the Bible and no
strong resonance with the mind of Christ in Scripture.

It would, therefore, be worth taking a closer look at Wesley's actual practice of the art. He recorded most of his reading after 1725,[8] and
this record runs to more than fourteen hundred different authors, with
nearly three thousand separate items from them (ranging from pam-
phlets to twelve-volume sets—including many huge leather bound
folios: sermons, histories, geography, voyages, and travels). He had had,
as we sometimes forget, a rich classical education and he kept this fur-
bished and in use throughout his whole career. His quotations—from
the classics or wherever—are rarely identified and rarely exact. And
they do sound a bit odd in our ears in what appear as sermons for mass
audiences.[9] Do you suppose, maybe, that mass audiences can take more
"culture" than we have condescendingly supposed (or are actually prepared to offer them)? At any rate, we have managed thus far, in the sermons alone, to identify twenty-seven quotations from Horace, many
of them repeated in different sermons.[10] Virgil follows with nineteen,[11]
Ovid with ten, Cicero with nine, and Juvenal seven. Twelve other classical authors[12] show up, repeatedly whenever they can serve, in support
(but sometimes also mere decoration) of one interesting point or
another. Wesley's other "classical" sources range from Plato to Aristotle
to Plotinus to Augustine to à Kempis. He knows the medieval mystics
and the Renaissance secularists (e.g., Rabelais). He quotes freely from
Shakespeare (once referring to him as "our heathen poet"[13]) and from
Milton even more freely—but also from Abraham Cowley, George
Herbert, Thomas Parnell, and Matthew Prior. He had read widely in

patristic theology, was well-grounded in the Reformation classics but was even more intimately acquainted with English "divinity," from Hooker to Baxter to Tillotson and Doddridge. His special anthology of "British divinity" appears, "extracted," in *A Christian Library*, but this is no more than a slice of a vaster bibliography to which he had exposed himself. One thing, therefore, is clear: if anybody proposes to theologize "in the Wesleyan spirit," he must learn to read and to *love* to read, to remember and to reflect—about all sorts of events and ideas in our human heritage and in our current world—as if he, too, were driven by the compulsions of an inquiring mind as Wesley was.

But literature was not the whole story of Wesley's culture by any means. He read all the "modern science" he could lay his hands on, with one eye on its theological import, and the other on its practical applications.[14] He had informed opinions about Newton and he soaked up the great popularizers of science in his day (Ray, Derham, Buddaeus, Goldsmith, and others) always supposing that whatever was true would help to illuminate God's glory in and through *his* creation. What often strikes one as odd, given our image of Wesley the evangelist, is the way in which he can comment on secular insights (especially in the later sermons) with no explicit evangelical reference for them (even though the biblical worldview is everywhere presupposed as self-evident). There are even some intriguing "off-limit" quotations (as a puritan might regard them) that expose his extensive acquaintance with English drama (including Restoration melodrama)—even while he was also denouncing the English theatre as a sinkhole of iniquity. For example, in 1726 he read Thomas Otway's *The Orphan, or The Unhappy Marriage*, written in 1680.[15] In 1759, one of the more telling quotations in Wesley's sermon on "Original Sin" is from Otway's *The Orphan*, Act V, Scene 1 (but, of course, with no citation). Now, did he keep that particular quotation in his head for thirty years; was it in his notes; or, had he reread Otway in the interim? I wish I knew. What is certain is that very few of his readers—then or since—have ever recognized the source of this quotation (or dozens like it). It was something of a detective feat for us to find it—and I use the pronoun *us* here quite literally, for in my search for these sources of Wesley's myriad uncited quotations, I have had the invaluable aid of Mrs. John Warnick[16] and Mrs. Wanda Smith (my research assistant).

All of this, however, was no more than an impressive superstructure set firmly upon a massive foundation of *biblical learning*, plus an incredible "information retrieval system" that reveals Wesley as a sort of walking concordance plus commentary, all in one. It was his profound sense of the Bible as a "speaking book" that gave him his freedom to "plunder the Egyptians" and guided him in the use he made of their treasures. One of the influences of the Holy Club on him was their collective emphasis upon Scripture as the primal authority that stands above and beyond all polarities and confessional formularies. In a letter to John Newton, April 24, 1765, Wesley says, "In 1730 I began to be *homo unius libri*, to study (comparatively) no book but the Bible."[17] In his preface to his first collection of *Sermons on Several Occasions* (1746) he avows his intention to be *homo unius libri* ("a man of just one book").[18] That "one book," of course, was Scripture and there can be no doubt at all that Wesley was, intentionally and in fact, a biblical man. All his basic insights are rooted in, or derived from, the Scriptures; he would often appeal "to the Law and the Testimony" as his court of last resort;[19] he would often urge his readers to weigh a difficult question "in the balance of the sanctuary" [i.e., in *prayerful* reflection upon the biblical data].[20] By *sola Scriptura* ("Scripture alone") he never meant "*nothing but Scripture*," just as by *unius libri* he never meant to exclude other books from his reading list—as we have already seen. But he did mean that Scripture was his first and final norm for the validation of any theological discussion. This meant a lifelong, total immersion in Scripture: in its original languages, in its dominant themes and images, in all its parts and in its organic wholeness. It was just this conviction that the Scripture insights are integral throughout, as a chorused witness to God's grace and human need, that allowed Wesley to range at will over the entire Bible and to conflate texts and paraphrases from here and there in sentences of his own in ways that are next to unimaginable to us nowadays—but that are neither unintelligible nor artificial (strange as that may seem). To verify this generalization experimentally, let me test it on you. Here are two (consecutive) sentences from his sermon on "Original Sin" (the one with the Otway quote mentioned above):

> *The Scripture avers, that by one man's disobedience, all men were constituted sinners; that in Adam all died, spiritually died, lost the life and the image of God; that fallen, sinful Adam then begat a son in his own likeness; nor was it possible he should beget him in any other, for who can bring a clean thing out of an unclean? That, consequently, we as well as other men, were by nature, dead in trespasses*

and sins, without hope, without God in the world, and
therefore children of wrath; [so] that every man may say, I
was shapen in wickedness, and in sin did my mother con-
ceive me; that there is no difference, in that all have sinned,
and come short of the glory of God, of that glorious image
of God, wherein man was originally created.[21]

Now, obviously, you can recognize that this language is, indeed, "biblical," but does it read as if it were "scissored-and-pasted"? Did you recognize that this passage, in its entirety, is composed of bits and pieces from Romans 5:19, 1 Corinthians 15:22, Genesis 5:3, Job 14:4, Ephesians 2:1, 12, and 3, Psalm 51:5, and then back home to Romans 3:22-23, in *that* order?

Let's try one more sample of this sort of thing that came to be a commonplace in Wesley's rhetoric (in his sermons, essays, letters, and treatises). There are hundreds of others like it that you can check out for yourself if you're interested—as I've come to be.

We are enabled by the Spirit to mortify the deeds of the
body, of our evil nature; and as we are more and more dead
to sin, we are more and more alive to God. We go on from
grace to grace, while we are careful to abstain from all appear-
ance of evil, and are zealous of good works as we have
opportunity, doing good to all men, while we walk in all His
ordinances blameless, therein worshipping Him in spirit and
in truth, while we take up our cross, and deny ourselves every
pleasure that does not lead us to God.[22]

What this adds up to is an obvious but crucial conclusion: Wesley *lived* in the Scriptures and his mind ranged over the Bible's length and breadth and depth like a radar, tuned into the pertinent data on every point he cared to make.

And yet this business of living in Scripture was not really what we have come to call "proof-texting" (i.e., the mechanical use of Scripture texts in support of some thesis or other that may or may not be truly "biblical," in its full context). Actually, these were only a few great basic themes that Wesley had discerned as the nerve centers of the biblical revelation and they guided him in both exegesis and hermeneutics. This becomes apparent as soon as you lay out all his recorded texts in various patterns and combinations. As some of you may know, Wesley kept a "Sermon Register" from 1747 to 1761. We have extended this to include every mention of any sermon and text anywhere else in the Wesley corpus and then have tried to organize these data into charts and generalizations that apply to his oral preaching as well as to his written sermons (published and manuscript). We are not at all certain that we yet have the full record: our 13,739 recorded texts fall short of the 40,000 some odd sermons attributed to him in his lifetime by some 26,000—in other words, by some two-thirds. Still, it must be the most nearly complete inventory of such statistics in existence and our efforts to analyze them are proving fruitful in many ways. For example, consider the text he used most often, 190 times: "Repent ye, and believe the gospel" (Mark 1:15). Then, combine that with Isaiah 55:6 and 55:7, "Seek ye the Lord while he may be found.... Let the wicked forsake his way, and the unrighteous man his thoughts: and let him return unto the Lord, and he will have mercy upon him; and to our God, for he will abundantly *pardon*," 90 and 112 times, respectively (i.e., 202 times together). Their sum (392 times) clearly suggests that Wesley's prime concern was the gospel call to repentance and the promise of pardon (and, remember that Isaiah was "gospel," too!). Look then at the next cluster of his overall favorites: (1) 2 Corinthians 8:9, "For ye know the grace of our Lord Jesus Christ, that, though he was rich, yet for your sakes he became poor, that ye through his poverty might be rich" (167 times); (2) Ephesians 2:8, "For by grace are ye saved through faith; and that not of yourselves: it is the gift of God" (133 times); and (3) Galatians 6:14, "But God forbid that I should glory, save in the cross of our Lord Jesus Christ, by whom the world is crucified unto me, and I unto the world" (129 times). From this it becomes evident that, for Wesley, the call to repentance was always linked with the gospel's offer of reconciliation through Christ and salvation by grace. His first six favorite texts, then, are all variations on the central evangelical message: *repent and accept God's grace in Christ!* There are many other fascinating patterns that have turned up in the course of our analyses of these texts—e.g., Wesley's favorite text in the first half-year of the Revival (1739) was 1 Corinthians 1:30, "But of him are ye in Christ Jesus, who of God is made unto us wisdom, and righteousness, and sanctification, and redemption" (12 times), and this was followed by Acts 16:30b, "What must I do to be saved?" (10 times). The following year (1740) his favorite text is the sixth chapter of Matthew (i.e., the central section of the Sermon on the Mount): 10 times. In 1741, his favorite text was Ephesians 2:8, "For by grace are ye saved through faith" (10 times) The New Testament books he preached from most often were Matthew (1,362 times), Hebrews (965 times) and John (910 times)—and he records no preaching texts from Philemon or 3 John. In the Old Testament Isaiah ranks first (668 times), Psalms second (624 times) and Jeremiah third (208 times), and he has left no record of ever having preached from the books of Ezra, Esther, Song of Solomon, Obadiah, or Nahum.

This (and much else I could lay out if space and time were no object) confirms the sincerity of Wesley's intention to live in the Bible as his theological climate. But this was matched by a comparable concern that his people also learn to live in and by the Scriptures in much the same way. For it was the interplay between Wesley's citations of Scripture and his people's familiarity with Scripture (however elementary) that so strongly reinforced the dynamics of his preaching and its impact. When a preacher has only a limited background in Scripture texts pondered deeply enough to support real biblical preaching and when his people have even less (or else a contrary hermeneutics), then one of the essential preconditions of effective Christian communication is missing—and this is enough in itself to account for many of our failures in effective pulpit communication today.

What I've been trying to suggest thus far is that Wesley was very much a man of his own time and yet also that his interest in the relevance of the perennial gospel in the constantly changing human situation is pertinent to our own efforts to update that same gospel and to relate it, as best we may, to the vast and radical crises of our times. One does not presume to stipulate exactly how Wesley would have diagnosed this current age. There is no doubt, however, that he would have *undertaken* a diagnosis, and we can suggest some of the fundamental principles he would have taken for his guidelines. At the heart of it all, then and now, is the over-arching issue that defined Christianity's crisis in the eighteenth century and that, in similar fashion, defines the crisis in which we are floundering in this latter half of the twentieth century: viz., human autonomy (freedom) versus heteronomy (oppression) on the one side (the human claim to our own control of our human destiny) and, over against these, Christian *theo*-nomy of one sort or another (human life lived intentionally by the righteousness and grace of God). In Wesley's day, the deists and French *philosophes* were the partisans of autonomy while secular tyrannies in variety represented the ancient traditions of social and political oppression. Wesley opposed both autonomy *and* heteronomy and sought instead a spiritual and social revolution in which *theo*-nomy provided both worldview and lifestyle for Christians: the love of God above all else and all else in God, reverence toward God, and the dignity of grace to *all* his children.

In our day—when all the great traditions that have held the world together for centuries (however tenuously) are suddenly becoming frazzled and "inoperative" —the issue between human self-sufficiency and God's primacy is still the great dividing line in all our struggles for a theology of culture that is actually *theo*-logy and not some sort of religious *anthro*-pology writ large across a cosmic backdrop. All our most fashionable credos today (the new a-morality, the new secularism, the new emotionalism and "supernaturalisms"—ESP, psychokinesis, "transcendental meditation," TA, and others) are all fresh variations on the old themes of human autonomy: viz., the conviction that human beings can and must accept final responsibility for their own well-being and their collective destinies. God, in this view, is at best a cosmic coach and, at worst, a pious fiction. Self-salvation is the implicit claim of all the self-help movements of our time—and not a few of the popular religious movements as well. But human autonomy, even partially achieved, attracts a counteraction from the right (viz., the management of our human affairs by other human beings— which is a working definition of heteronomy). Thus we may venture into prophecy: when a society that has been enchanted by the visions of self-salvation becomes disenchanted (or comes under the sorts of social and economic duress we are now experiencing), that society is sadly vulnerable to secular tyranny. For anyone to fail to see that *this* is the agonizing issue at the heart of our progressive disintegration as a nation for the past two decades is a strange form of moral blindness. What is worse, the choice between autonomy and heteronomy is humanly intolerable in the long run. Autonomy is a delusion and heteronomy is a degradation. Is this what folk like Solzhenitsyn have been trying to tell us?

It is, therefore, clearly in the Wesleyan spirit for Christians (ministers and laity alike) to explore the terms in which God's primacy and sovereign grace may once again be affirmed and translated into convincing witness and service in this world as it exists and as it runs its course. But, even supposing that we could, in reasonable measure, master this ancient art of plundering the Egyptians, how on earth would we put such resources to fruitful use?

There is no easy answer here. Christian ministers in our day, as we know all too well, are struggling in the throes of a deep identity crisis. They are no longer "the parsons" of their town or city and thus are no longer decisively influential in public affairs, *ex officio*. But if they turn, in desperation or relief, to some other sort of service profession—as "public relations persons," amateur journalists or editors, paramedical "shrinks," or even professors—they are still without a truly distinctive "office," with no indispensable *professional* role in this new society of ours. Whatever such amateurs can do, in those various roles and functions, professionals can do as well or better. But what none of them can do as well as good ministers, who really know their calling (who understand its resources in Scripture and tradition together with its art of transvaluating secular wisdoms into Christian insights), is to bring the gospel to bear on the living, aching concerns of contemporary men and women in their daily round, in the terms of their specific current cultural perceptions. The only really distinctive thing the Christian minister has to offer—in its appropriate cultural context—is the Christian gospel in its full essence, replete with its promises to transform and hallow human lives and human culture. The fundamentalist or liberal who is either antipathetic to a given current culture or out of touch with it—no matter how devout, or "biblical," or ecstatic or "activist"—cannot really do this. The impact of such "sectarians" on history and on society is either marginal or short-lived. But the *evangelical* Christian must also have an ample grasp and evaluation of the culture and times in which one lives (a vivid sense of tradition—the human past—together with a realistic sense of the human prospect). This is one's "Egyptian plunder" and one must take careful, constant thought as to how it may be exploited most effectively in preaching and teaching—else one will not be preaching the *full* gospel, either, no matter what one's advertising "logo" may be.

This, or something like it, is what Wesley understood as "theological education" and what he insisted on from his preachers, ignoring their general lack of *formal* education. His first question was always about a person's "gifts, graces, and fruits"—one's commitment to Christ and to the Scriptures' witness as God's Word and our Savior. But he then also asked about each person's willingness to learn and his/her aptness for study and teaching. His curriculum for "continuing education" would certainly stretch most of *us*.[23]

This enterprise—of living in Scripture and on the growing edge of the human situation in any given age—is a formidable, demanding task, not one for the fainthearted or the slothful. But the true Wesleyan will settle for nothing less in a personal program for professional growth and development. It means living in the Scripture, not as a crossword puzzle for exegetes but as a font of inspiration and—

yes, *revelation*! It means learning to think *biblically*. Furthermore, it means learning to live in the Christian past so that you can appropriate the lessons already learned by Christians in other times and circumstances, in their struggles for "a true gospel for *this* age" (whenever that "age" may have been). It means alertness and sensitivity to every new cultural development on the human horizon, without becoming "trendy" or falling easy prey to "every passing wind of doctrine" (cf. Eph. 4:14). It means profound reliance upon that inner nourishment of soul and mind that comes from the inner witness of the Holy Spirit—"no craven spirit but one that inspires us to strength, love and self-discipline" (as is well-said in 2 Timothy 1:17, NEB). Something like this is what is implied in taking Wesley (or Calvin or Augustine or Origen before him) as model or example. This is what is implied by our rich metaphor of "plundering the Egyptians."

Speaking practically, any such commitment involves an agenda of incessant reading, constant reflection, unquenchable curiosity, a restless quest for new perspectives, new alternatives to everything that is merely commonplace or to all reckless extremes on either side of each live issue. Remember that Wesley read as he rode, thought as he wrote, ruminated as he rested—that he was neither a harried man nor a self-pitying one. Thus, we can learn from him what it takes to combine a life of prayer and worship, of preaching and pastoral care, with a healthy curiosity about the world in which we minister. By precept and example, he could teach us what "inward" and "outward" holiness means: an outreach toward the perfecting of our love of God, plus a comparable love for all our neighbors that implies permanent social revolution. There are better and worse ways to implement this Wesleyan program—and we could usefully debate the alternatives in our own proposals for continuing education—alternatives seeking to translate our Wesleyan models into meaningful programs of our own. What matters for us is to realize that *something like this* belongs to the very essence of theologizing in the Wesleyan spirit: keeping our witness to Christ in active dialogue with this world in which he is to be proclaimed, this world for which he died. And if such a program is an "impossible possibility" (in Reinhold Niebuhr's famous phrase), then what more valid ideal could we ever set for ourselves? What less ought thoughtful laity ask of their pastors?

It is in some such spirit as this that I believe we can conceive of a truly Wesleyan way of doing theology nowadays—with open eyes to our heritage and our future, both within the wide, loving providence of God. These next three chapters are, therefore, offered as experiments (sketchy but serious) in recovering and updating the Wesleyan theology in this spirit, insofar as I see now how this might be done. My proposal, therefore, is to take Wesley's three central themes and to rehearse them in a way that I hope will be recognized as faithful to Wesley and yet also in an idiom that can be recognized as "contemporary." The ruling premise throughout is my conviction that every thoughtful Christian must accept responsibility for the overcoming of polarities without compromise, for affirming pluralism without drifting into indifferentism, for learning to live in the Scripture, the Christian past, and modern world all at once. And whatever its perplexities, we ought to think of any such project as an up reaching aspiration that will be sustained by the upholding grace of our Lord Jesus Christ, the unfailing love of God our Father, in the continuing communion and fellowship of his Holy Spirit.

In the midst of the Revival, Wesley took time out to try to describe this business of theology and culture ("plundering the Egyptians") – in what he meant to be a curriculum, or sorts, for continuing theological education. We may find it dated in some respects, yet I hope you will agree with me that it still has real relevance for us and for others like us. It is entitled *An Address to the Clergy* (1756)[24] and I offer you a test sampling from it as a way of confirming and concluding what I've been trying to say thus far. The well-furnished minister, says Wesley, must have "a capacity for reasoning with some closeness," "a lively turn of thought," "a good memory," "a competent share of knowledge." Then comes Scripture (in the original tongues), plus "a knowledge of history, . . . of sciences, . . . metaphysics, . . . natural philosophy, . . . the history of Christian thought and devotion, . . . a knowledge of the [contemporary] world . . ." To knowledge and culture must be added "common sense, . . ." and "the animations of grace in one's affections and daily rounds": a clear sense of calling and a principled indifference to the blandishments of greed and ambition.

> *Brethren [says he in conclusion], is not this our calling . . .?*
> *And why (I will not say do we fall short, but why) are we satisfied with falling so far short of it? Is there any necessity laid upon us of sinking so infinitely below our calling? . . . Why then may not you be as "burning and shining lights" as those that have shone [before you]? Do you desire to partake of the same burn-*

ing love, of the same shining holiness? Surely you do. You cannot but be sensible it is the greatest blessing which can be bestowed [on us]. . . . Then, as the Lord liveth, ye shall attain. . . . Then, assuredly, "the great Shepherd" of us and our flocks will "make us perfect in every good work to do his will, and work in us all that is well pleasing in his sight"! This is the desire and prayer of

Your Brother and Servant,
in our common Lord,
John Wesley

London, February 6, 1756.

II: Diagnosing the Human Flaw: Reflections Upon the Human Condition

ne of Wesley's ambitions, never realized, was to bring all the English evangelicals, Church of England and Dissenters, into an active alliance. The Dissenters rejected him because of his Anglican loyalties; the Anglicans ostracized him because of his irregular churchmanship. Many in both camps argued that he had pared his list of Christian essentials too close to the bone. And it *was* a short list: "(1) original sin, (2) justification by faith alone, and (3) holiness of heart and life."[1] Here are the three central pillars of Wesleyan theology and I propose to represent them, *seriatim*. Let us begin, therefore, with "*original sin*."

When was the last time you preached, or heard, a sermon on "original sin"? How many of you would take seriously the notion of a human flaw that is radical, inescapable, universal—a human malaise that cannot be cured or overcome by any of our self-help efforts or ethical virtues, however "moral" or aspiring—which is not, at the same time, of the actual essence of God's original design for the *humanum* (what he intended human existence to be)? How many of you are inclined to take seriously the old "articles" on "sin" in our various "confessions" and "articles of religion"?[2] Have you ever tried to reformulate this ancient doctrine in contemporary terms that conserve its valid intentions, supposing that you grant that its intentions are still valid? I still remember a lanky West Texas Pelagian in one of my first classes here who came by the office to complain that I *sounded* as if human sinning were something deeper and more mysterious than a failure of free will or a moral lapse. Such a strange idea intrigued him and he asked for suggestions for further reading. At the time, John Whale's *Christian Doctrine* was newly published, so I mentioned that. To his credit, he went off and found Whale, but was back again a fortnight later still more baffled—since Whale, as some of you know, was a good deal more of a "classical Protestant" on this point than I have ever been. We talked about it a while and finally he gave vent to a real outcry from his heart: "Well," said he, "if we don't have the power to *decide* to sin or *decide* not to sin, then all I've got to say is, 'God help us!'" This, of course, was an obvious cue for pointing out that he had unwittingly betrayed himself into involuntary orthodoxy!

For the crux of this whole ancient, vexed problem is precisely the Pelagian contention that man is able to sin or not to sin as he chooses—so that if and when humans become aware that given acts are sinful, they are free, in their natural moral agency, to decide to go ahead ("for the hell of it") or else to inhibit their behavior. Here is the swirling vortex of centuries of controversy, and the passage between its two extremes is booby-trapped on both sides. For if you argue that we are sinful by nature (i.e., that the power only to sin is the actual human condition), you are also on the verge of saying that the original sin is simply being human—and that's heresy. If you take the opposite side, and argue that we *can* banish sin from our own lives and societies whenever we muster up sufficient moral effort (prodded inwardly by conscience and outwardly by moral example and admonition), you are on the verge of saying that sin is, in essence, a sort of social dysfunction, corrigible by moral insight and effort, or by proper programs of social reform. If you then persist in arguing for *original* sin, in some sense or other, you may be implying that we are sort of badly botched animals since, clearly, no other animal "sins" with anything like the same regularity, recklessness, and tragic consequence as does the human animal. But this is heresy as well—for it denies the moral uniqueness of the human creation.

Now, the obvious "gospel" for people able not to sin if they so will—to sin or not to sin, *that* is the question!—is salvation by moral rectitude. This, however stated, is in reality a gospel of *self*-salvation. According to this formula, it is self-understanding and self-direction that make up the recipe for human happiness. The gospel for the radically sinful, on the other hand, must say something about one's justification by God (which is to say, salvation) as a divine initiative to which we humans may respond. God in Christ, so this gospel goes, has taken the initiative in overcoming the ruptured relations between himself and his alienated children. On Lutheran grounds, for example, it runs something like this: "You (or some of you) are accepted by God because of Christ's merits, despite all your moral defects. Accept God's acceptance of you, indomitable concupiscence and all. This is what faith means: to accept God's sheer unmerited favor ["just as I am, without one plea"]. You will still be *simul justus et peccator*—justified before God and still a sinner all at the same time—but your being justified by grace is what really counts." Lutherans are careful to leave open the question as to why some people accept their acceptance while so many others apparently do not.

Properly instructed Calvinists start from the same premise—that sin is radical and that justification is by divine fiat. Then they proceed with quite different nuances in the development of their doctrines of the Christian life. Some sinners—utterly undeserving of God's mercy, utterly unable to save themselves—may, by God's free election, have the righteousness of Christ *imputed* to them and so come to be regarded as righteous by God for Christ's sake, having no righteousness of their own to plead. This notion of *election* ("predestination") has three concomitant notions in traditional Calvinist soteriology: (1) limited atonement (since it is clear that the mass of humanity is not elected, in point of fact); (2) irresistible grace (else God's free election could be nullified); and (3) final perseverance (since God's will cannot finally be thwarted). This is the famous TULIP[3] syndrome and can be seen in its starkest form in the so-called "Lambeth Articles" of 1595 (drafted by William Whitaker, opposed by Peter Baro—*before* the Arminian controversy and *long before* the Synod of Dort). These "articles" are worth "resurrecting" here, for while they cannot be familiar to many moderns, Wesley knew them well and had studied the issues in the long, bitter controversy that stretched from Cartwright and Hooker to his own day.[4]

> 1. God from eternity hath predestinated certain men unto life; certain men he hath reprobated.
> 2. The moving or efficient cause of predestination unto life is not the foresight of faith, or of perseverance, or of good works, . . . but only the good will and pleasure of God.
> 3. There is predetermined a certain number of the pre-destinate, which can neither be augmented nor diminished.

4. Those who are not predestinated to salvation shall be necessarily damned for their sins.

5. A true, living, and justifying faith, and a sanctifying by the Spirit of God is not extinguished, . . . it vanisheth not away in the elect, either finally or totally.

6. A man . . . who is endued with a justifying faith is certain, with the full assurance of faith, of the remission of his sins and of his everlasting salvation by Christ.

7. Saving grace is . . . not granted, is not communicated, to all men, by which they may be saved *if they will.*

8. No man can come unto Christ unless it shall be given unto him, and unless the Father shall draw him; and all men are not drawn by the Father, that they may come to the Son.

9. It is not in the will or power of every one to be saved.[5]

This statement was approved in a conference in Lambeth Palace, subscribed by the Archbishop of Canterbury (Dr. Whitgift) and approved by the Archbishop of York (Dr. Hutton). They were then quietly nullified by "Good Queen Bess" under the urging of Bishop Bancroft of London. This was the high-water mark for the cause of "high" Calvinism in the Church of England and it played its part in Wesley's lifelong bias against predestination. But the trouble was that, by Wesley's time, the Calvinists had appropriated the label "evangelical" to themselves alone—so that justification by faith and the TULIP syndrome had come to be identified by most English Christians as mutual implicates. Most of the alternative positions had been lumped together under the label "Arminianism," and this was generally identified with the gospel of moral rectitude. We shall have to look more closely at Wesley's so-called "Arminianism" as we go along.

Now, any doctrine of sin and depravity as a diagnosis of the human condition is a paradox. Few will deny that there is a lot of sinning (or at the very least, deplorable behavior) in the world. But whether it is "original" or some sort of social dysfunction—the fruitage of unevolved animal residues or a distinctively *human* flaw—is a thorny question with no clear, neat answers (except the wrong ones!). Why *should* we sin unless we are driven to it by demons or neurosis? Why can't we point to a single fully human and humane society, somewhere on this planet—moral, just, peaceable? We have no difficulty in idealizing such a human possibility. Obviously, we have very impressive moral potentials. Most of us have consciences to enforce our ego and social ideals, up to a point. Is it true, then, as St. Paul claims, "that when I want to do the right, only the wrong is within my reach"? Is it true (as he goes on to add) that "in my inmost self I delight in the law of God, but I also perceive a different law in my bodily members, fighting against the law that my reason approves, making me a prisoner under the law . . . of sin"?[6] And if this is *not* true, how else will we account for the amplitude, universality and tragedy of our failures to attain to God's moral design for human happiness? Why is there so much of "man's inhumanity to man"? Our answers, whatever they may be, are the nucleus of our doctrines of original sin. This, in turn, will help to shape one's doctrine of justification (by faith *or* good works). *That*, in turn, will affect all one's notions of the Christian life: how it is entered, how Christians mature, what our Christian hopes may be—here and hereafter. This, then, will direct our vision of "salvation"—i.e., the terms of human fulfillment and human happiness. This question about sin ("original" sin at that) is not, therefore, just an abstract speculation. It plagues *us* as agonizingly as it did Wesley. Something *has* gone fearfully awry in the human enterprise. Everywhere (and in our own hearts!) we see the signs of this tragic discrepancy between our visions of what human existence ought to be and what it actually ever is. But what is the human potential—and why do we fall short of it, all of us, one way or another? No one can live responsibly or help others to live responsibly without thoughtful answers to these questions—*now!*

How John Wesley came to his own mature doctrine of the human flaw—and to a gospel that could match it—is a complicated story that I have only recently begun to think I can sort out (since the conventional accounts of it have never seemed quite credible). He says, more than once, that the doctrine of justification by faith alone was a novelty to him before 1738, and to many others in the Church of England as well.[7] This cannot have been literally true, for he could not have studied theology in Oxford from 1720 to 1735 without becoming aware of the famous controversy on this very point (Downham and Davenant *vs.* Taylor and Hammond, John Bunyan *vs.* Richard Baxter, *et al.*),[8] to say nothing of the official statements in the Thirty-Nine Articles and the Homilies to which he had subscribed. What he meant was that he had grown up with the gospel of moral rectitude, and that this was the dominant view in Anglican soteriology as he knew it. The premise of such a gospel was the human moral ability to sin only by choice. Its prescription for the Christian life, therefore, was moral effort, encouraged, sanctioned, and rewarded by the church (through her "means of grace"). It included the doctrines of baptismal regeneration and a sacramental life that, in some sense, guaranteed grace. His early sermons[9]—together with his very interesting theological discussions with his mother (his first and best theological tutor)—all reflect an earnest dedication of his life and labors to the high goals of holy living, holy dying and of Christian happiness in God, not the world. Two of its manuals (favorites in the Epworth rectory) were Lorenzo Scupoli's *Spiritual Struggle*[10] and Henry Scougal's *The Life of God in the Soul of Man*.[11] It is not only unfair, but misleading, to depreciate the Christian intentions enshrined in this gospel of moral rectitude. The Methodist stereotypes of irreligious Anglican parsons have their grain of truth but are obviously also self-serving (to inflate Methodist egos); they ignore the spiritual achievements of eighteenth century Anglicanism. The *real* problem with this doctrine of a moral ability not to sin except at will (for Wesley and for all its other adherents then and ever since) was the tragic discrepancy between its promises and performance. For all his zeal and devotion—in Oxford and Epworth and Georgia—he never found the happiness or the serenity that the holy living tradition advertised. The Holy Club was not "a happy club." The refugee missionary from Georgia was a miserable victim of his own frustrated ideals.

Even so, the alternative offered him by the Moravians and Salzburgers in Georgia and, later, by Peter Böhler in England was hard to take—and this is what made Aldersgate so dramatic an event that it has overshadowed the larger theological mutation that took place *throughout* the year 1738 (beginning with his shipboard memorandum of Tuesday, January 24th,[12] through the formation of the Religious Society at Fetter Lane on May 1st,[13] Aldersgate itself,[14] the visit to Germany, June 14th to September 16th,[15] Wesley's discovery of Jonathan Edwards's *Faithful Narrative* on October 9th,[16] and finally, his production of *The Doctrine of Salvation, Faith and Good Works, Extracted from the Homilies of the Church of England* [November 12th]).[17] What really matters is that, by that year's end, he had made a decisive switch from the gospel of moral rectitude to "justification by faith alone" (*sola fide*)—i.e., to a doctrine of a radical, universal human flaw—from all talk about human merit to radical trust in God's pardon as a *gift*, in and through the merits of Christ's mediatorial sacrifice. The Aldersgate story in the *Journal* is very carefully reconstructed so as to focus the convergence of two great Christian traditions that had been in painful tension ("holy living" and faith alone) upon one single "moment" in a single place, after two centuries of conflict. This is why its climax is so readily misconstrued when isolated from the account as a whole. How many of us have traced out Wesley's careful *background* analysis of his heartwarming? Or, again, how many have pondered that later *Journal* entry of January 4, 1739, where he says of himself: "But that I am not a Christian *at this day* [seven months *after* Aldersgate] I as assuredly know as that Jesus is the Christ."[18]

The essence of the Aldersgate experience was a sudden new assurance that "I did trust in Christ, Christ alone, for salvation . . . that Christ had taken away my sins, even mine, and had saved me from the law of sin and death." This was Wesley's personal appropriation of the classical Protestant diagnosis of the human plight along with the classical Protestant gospel of "faith alone," *sola fide*. Its presupposition was a stress on the human flaw as radical (incurable by any human effort or merit). *This* was the sense in which Wesley could claim (as he did) that, on the point of justification by faith alone, he stood no more than a hair's breadth from Calvin—or any other true "evangelical."[19]

Real trouble began—and here's where the plot of Wesleyan theologizing really begins to thicken!—when he balked at going further and accepting the entire Protestant package. The first breach was with the Moravians and their Lutheran doctrine of invincible concupiscence. Then, *vis-à-vis* the Calvinists, he rejected the last four of their "five points." This was less a deliberate decision than an intractable bias against election, irresistible grace and final perseverance—because of what he took to be their moral (i.e., antinomian) implications. On the other side, his all-out advocacy of original sin and justification by faith alone had the effect of cutting him off from most of his Anglican contemporaries. His instinctive rejection of quietism wore out his earlier welcome with the Moravians. This helps to explain why the Wesleyan revival was so nearly a one-man operation and why no latitudinarians and very few "evangelical" Anglicans would cooperate with him or support his segment of the movement. The Dissenters wanted no part of his commitment to the Church of England as a comprehensive sacramental community. The resultant "third alternative" was an interesting—and original—anomaly (viz., a Protestant doctrine of original sin minus most of the other elements in classical Protestant soteriology, *plus* a catholic doctrine of perfection *without* its full panoply of priesthood and priestcraft).[20] Thus, he stood exposed to charges of inconsistency from both sides. Even after justification by faith alone had become his central message, he retained the holy living tradition of his upbringing and he taught his people not only to go on toward perfection but to "expect to be made perfect in love in this life"! This caught him in a crossfire—a catholic who had become an evangelical and yet never ceased to be catholic: i.e., an evangelical-catholic! This was an ecumenical move of prime importance—and could be even more relevant today than then, because now it just might be more fully appreciated by more people, if it were really understood (and if we could ever get Wesley rescued from his too-exclusive Methodist identification and recognized for the ecumenical theologian that he was and meant to be).

The critical nuance here is the difference in his doctrine of "original sin" and "total depravity" from what Gilbert Rowe taught me to call "*tee*-total depravity" (i.e., the Lutheran and Calvinist diagnoses of the human condition). The twofold clue here is in (1) Wesley's (essentially catholic) view of sin as a malignant *disease* rather than an obliteration of the *imago Dei* in fallen human nature, and (2) in his displacement of the doctrine of "election" with the notion of "prevenient grace." He could have gotten his particular doctrine of prevenience from Bellarmine, for he is closer to Bellarmine *on this point* than to Calvin—and we know that he had read Bellarmine's *De Justificatione* and the history of the Roman Catholic controversy over grace and free will between the Jesuits and Dominicans. But a more obvious source for "prevenience," in this sense, was his own Anglican tradition.[21] In any case, this is one of the "new" questions that Roman Catholics and Anglicans and Methodists ought to explore together, with a few Lutherans and Calvinists thrown into the mix to keep everybody honest. The old chasms between Protestants and Catholics on sin and free will, and on justification and grace, have altered their form and substance in the past two decades or so, and it would be fruitful for Wesley's ideas about sin and grace to be included in any serious reconsideration of the problem at this new stage of the dialogue.

His driving passion was to find a third alternative to Pelagian optimism and Augustinian pessimism with respect to the human flaw and the human potential. In his early gospel of moral rectitude, original sin (as an entail of Adam's fall) was washed away in baptismal regeneration, leaving behind a "tinderbox of sin" (the *fomes peccati*) together with a residual moral ability to sin or not sin, as one might choose. And if one chose to sin, one could still repent, bring forth fruits meet for repentance and be assured of God's pardon, by the church (on the basis of her "power of the keys"). The crucial aim in this tradition was to hold persons responsible for their deeds and misdeeds, and to stifle amoralisms of every kind. Its proposed remedy for the human flaw (and Wesley's, too, before 1738) was dual: (1) earnest moral effort, guided by the church; and (2) faithful use of the means of grace which the church alone supplies. This optimism, of course, was undercut by any truly *radical* doctrine of sin, as one can realize from the Duchess of Buckingham's toplofty complaint to the Countess of Huntingdon (an evangelical blue blood all the way!):

> *I thank your ladyship for the information concerning the Methodist preachers. Their doctrines are most repulsive and strongly tinctured with impertinence and disrespect towards their superiors, in perpetually endeavouring to level all ranks and do away with all distinctions. It is monstrous to be told that you have a heart as sinful as the common wretches that crawl the earth.*[22]

A somewhat more substantial denial of all notions of sin as radical came from Dr. John Taylor of Norwich. In a famous book in 1740, he argued that men do sin (obviously!), but they *could* do otherwise, and they should be guided and admonished to do so. "They can do their duty *if* they choose!" Taylor's blithe confidence in human autonomy struck Wesley as profoundly unbiblical and anti-evangelical—and he reacted quickly with the longest piece he ever wrote: *The Doctrine of Original Sin, According to Scripture, Reason and Experience.*[23] Then, in 1759, he digested "Part I" of the treatise into a sermon that was then placed first in volume IV of the *Sermons* (1760). In both treatise and sermon, Wesley takes the Protestant hard line, asserting the utter impotence of man's *natural* moral powers. Fallen man was (and is) "by *nature* purely evil . . . unmixed with anything of an opposite nature . . . He never deviated into good"!

In our naturally sinful condition, we "have no more significant knowledge of God than the beasts of the field . . . Having no proper knowledge of God we have no love of him . . . Every man born into the world is a rank idolater . . . We have set up our idols in our hearts, . . . we worship ourselves . . . We seek happiness in the creature, instead of the Creator." This doctrine, he goes on to insist, "is the first distinguishing point between heathenism and Christianity." In pagan morality (and in natural morality) the presupposition is that "the natural good much overbalances the evil. Christianity [on the other hand] makes sin a shibboleth: 'Is man by nature filled with all manner of evil? Is he void of all good? Is he wholly fallen? Is his soul totally corrupted?' . . . Allow this and you are so far a Christian. Deny it and you are but a heathen still."

This is a grim picture and verges on the Augustinian-Calvinist extreme. And yet (and there's always a "not-yet" whenever Wesley tilts toward any extreme), he immediately yokes the doctrine of total depravity with its antidote (where "total" means that *all* of the *humanum* is "depraved," rather than that none of it is anything but depraved): (1) God's own *therapeia psyches* (his *curative* activity within our hearts) and (2) God's universally active initiative in calling sinners to authentic repentance and self-knowledge. This is pre-venient and here is where "prevenient" grace functions as an alternative to *election*. Sin is spoken of as a sickness that can be cured by the Great Physician if we will accept his threefold prescription: (1) repentance (self-knowledge), (2) renunciation of self-will, and (3) faith (trust in God's sheer, unmerited grace). "The great end of religion is to renew our hearts in the image of God, to repair that total loss of righteousness and true holiness which we sustained by the sin of our first parents."[24]

What is original here is Wesley's stout upholding of the sovereignty of grace but not its irresistibility—and this distinction deserves more pondering than it usually gets. Sinners can do literally nothing to save themselves (not by merit, nor demerit, nor by the will to believe). And yet God's intention in creating persons (which gives each person his/her unique identity) is not thwarted by human resistance, because it is God's own purpose that the offer of grace shall be experienced *as optional*. The chief function of prevenient grace, therefore, is to stir the sinner to repentance (which is to say, to a valid self understanding of his/her sinfulness). Thus, Wesley can speak of repentance as the *porch* of religion, of faith as the *door*, and of holiness as religion itself.[25]

What happens in repentance is a sort of self-recognition that identifies spiritual pride and self-righteousness and rejects them both as inauthentic. This allows us to realize that it is God, for Christ's sake, who can and who has forgiven all our sins and broken the power of sin and death in our hearts. Thus, it is repentance that also calls us to faith and to that trust in God that alters the basis of our existence.

It is just here that Wesley takes a turn away from the classical Protestant soteriology. Luther and Calvin regarded the residue of sin (*fomes peccati*) not only as ineradicable but sinful as such; it falls under God's righteous condemnation even though this does not forfeit his justifying grace. Wesley distinguishes between "sin properly so-called" (i.e., a conscious, deliberate violation of a known law of God) and *involuntary* sins and misdeeds. This, obviously, presupposes that residual sin (*fomes peccati*) diminishes in force and influence as the Christian grows in grace. There *are* "wandering thoughts,"[26] and these must be sent packing. There is "sin in believers"[27] and this must be repented of, promptly. "Sin *remains* but no longer *reigns*."[28] Those who are justified by faith alone are led, by the Holy Spirit in their consciences, to discover "new" sins, or their sinful abuses of innocent human aspirations—and to recognize temptations which, if entertained seriously enough to form moral intentions, will result in the forfeiture of one's justification.[29] This notion of the Christian way as forever perilous offended the Calvinists' reliance upon "final perseverance." It seemed to them as if Wesley's God was unable to keep his own elect unto the day of their salvation. For Wesley, however, it was just this double notion of sin as reducible and of faith as a risky business that reinforced his stress on Christian self-discipline (moral *and* spiritual). For as the believer learns to repent daily, and to trust God's grace, and to grow in that grace, then he begins to move from the threshold of faith (justification) toward its fullness (sanctification). This particular linkage between *sola fide* (justification) and "holy living" (sanctification) has no precedent, to my knowledge, anywhere in classical Protestantism.

For our purposes in updating the Wesleyan tradition for these times, a good deal of Wesley's rhetoric and conceptual apparatus may safely be left back there with the rest of his eighteenth century culture. Literal notions of Adam's fall or of the seminal transmission of sin and guilt are unintelligible to the modern mind, even when it tries to think biblically. The essence of human sin is not the helpless repetition of Adam's act—even though there *is* an analogue here for understanding how insatiable our human hungers for a knowledge of good and evil really are. Sin is not our actual misdeeds, nor even the evil impulses that still lurk in the murky depths of the human heart. Sin, in its essence, is human *overreach*—the reckless abuse of our distinctive human outreachings and upreachings—those aspirations that make us human but whose corruptions make us less than truly human. Sin is the bitter fruit of pride. It springs from our intimations of the infinite and our desires to avoid or escape the actual terms of our finite existence. Sin is our unwillingness to be radically dependent upon God "for life and breath and all things." It is, therefore, the idolatry of preferring to be "gods" rather than truly human (which was, of course, the primal temptation in Eden).

The fruit of sin is *bondage* (i.e., slavery to our own self-deceptions, to our illusions about life and society that stir up utopias that never quite transpire). The result of our overreaching in each of our distinctively human outreaches does not bring the real self-satisfaction that we keep on expecting, but rather tragic self-stultification instead (and for this there is no fully rational or even morally acceptable explanation—since our self-excuses do not finally satisfy).

For example, an overreaching aspiration to freedom, if successful, presently tempts one to the *abuse* of his freedom and to a denial of that freedom to others. Groups that achieve liberation slide almost unwittingly into oppressions of their own. Overreaching intelligence turns into intellectual arrogance. Overreaching aspirations to self-knowledge and self-control turn into narcissism and self-deception. Joy that is snatched at, or clung to, is tainted by transience, and brings on nostalgia or depression—or else to redoubled efforts to be happy, none of them with anything approaching lasting satisfaction. Human love is forever overreaching itself—it is incontinent by nature (that is its glory and misery). It never willingly comes to terms with the brackets of finitude, symbolized most harshly by death. This is "human bondage."

In the Old Testament, the phrase "house of bondage" connotes both Egyptian slavery and also the sinful state of humanity.[30] Paul uses the phrase "the spirit of bondage" as a synonym for sin.[31] The human flaw and this spirit of bondage are, in this sense, paired metaphors for the human abuse of the human potential for creative freedom *and* also the tragic consequences of such abuses in the frail textures of a humane society.

But there is no *necessity* for this, no divine purpose that compels such creatures as we were meant to be to have become the creatures that we are. There is no *good* reason why human outreach *has* to overreach itself. Sin and sinners cannot, therefore, justify or excuse themselves. *This* is "the mystery of iniquity"[32] which we need to ponder alongside "the mystery of godliness."[33] If the human flaw inheres in our merely being human, then every promise of salvation is some sort of legal fiction which will never satisfy our hunger for true and full humanity. If, on the other hand, sin is merely social dysfunction, then it ought in principle to be corrigible and salvation ought really to be possible by some formula or program of self-salvation or group-salvation. And yet in the long history of social activism there is no evidence whatever that persons or groups or societies have ever achieved their full human potential by means of human wisdom or heroism or even "letting be" (save on some relative scale of amelioration that always falls short of our proper human hunger for the utmost). Nor is there any credible prospect for it, apart from the euphoric visions of our currently fashionable "human potential" optimists.

Our real dilemma lies deeper—in this tragic welter of aspirations that corrupt each other. "O, wretched man that I am" (Rom. 7:24)—even if I have learned the newly sacrosanct Pelagian litany, "I'm O.K., You're O.K.!" The fact of the human tragedy is everywhere and inescapable—in lives whose humanity is denied or despoiled by others, in lives that reach out for happiness and yet are mocked by disappointment, doomed to death. Who or what could possibly deliver us from this primordial tragedy without robbing us of our freedom and thus also of our full humanity? The only answer I can think of (or have ever heard of), not already clearly falsified in human experience itself over the decades and centuries, is some sort of active intervention in our lives and in our human history by that purpose and power of whatever or whoever it was that ever intended us to be free and joyous and loving to begin with.

Is there such a power or purpose or person? Is there any such intention that is in fact our human destiny? Whatever we have to say to questions like these had better contain all the clues in our faith and all the insights that have turned up in our efforts to help God's prodigal sons and daughters find their way back home to the Father's house. Wesley had some thoughts on this, too, as one might expect, and those thoughts and their possible relevance for our efforts to understand and communicate the gospel, will furnish us with grist for further comment.

III: On "Offering Christ": The Gist of the Gospel

e have been speaking of the human flaw, and of its bitter fruit in human bondage. But is there an honest answer to the anguished question, "Who shall deliver us *from* this bondage?" Wesley thought there was. His whole career was an astonishing demonstration of a gospel that effected a Christian revolution in his time and society, and for a full century afterwards. In a hundred different ways on thousands of different occasions, decade after five decades, his one consistent message was Jesus Christ and him crucified—*Christus crucifixus, Christus redemptor, Christus victor*. First Corinthians 1:30 was one of his favorite texts (72 times altogether) and, as we noted above, his favorite single text during the first crucial half-year of the Revival.[1]

For example, on July 17th of that year, he came to Bath where he fell into a casual disputation with a gentleman who remembered his Oxford reputation for being "a little crack-brained." "However [Wesley goes on] some persons who were not of his mind, having pitched on a convenient place . . . on top of the hill under which the town lies, I there *offered Christ* to about a thousand people for 'wisdom, righteousness, sanctification and redemption' [1 Cor. 1:30]. Thence I returned to Bath and preached on 'What must I do to be saved?' [Acts 16:30b] to a larger audience than ever before."[2]

The burden of his evangelical message was always the same, the references are almost monotonous. He speaks of "preaching Christ," of "offering Christ," proclaiming Christ," "declaring Christ,"[3] and so forth. And always it was the gospel of salvation by grace through faith, justification and deliverance through God's grace in Christ. It was a projection—across half a century and three kingdoms—of his discovery at Aldersgate, his unwavering conviction that the essence of authentic Christian experience is trusting Christ, Christ alone, for salvation, a trust that generates an inward "assurance . . . that Christ has taken away *my* sins, even *mine*, and has saved *me* from the law of sin and death."[4]

Time was, as we know, when *evangelical* and *evangelism* were dirty words for liberals in general—and this included, as a matter of course, the majority of the Methodists (at least the clergy). We thought we had outgrown nineteenth century revivalism and the sort of private piety that clings to Jesus and ignores the human agonies of this world, this world for which Christ died. To this day, there is a sort of litmus paper test of a person's theological reactions and type. If you can hear (or sing)

> *Jesus paid it all,*
> *All to him I owe,*
> *Sin had left a crimson stain,*
> *He washed it white as snow,*

with serious meaning and without queasiness, you're either not as liberal as you thought or else somebody has been tampering with your liberalism. Either way, the test will serve as an indication that the whole problem of justification by faith alone is still in unresolved confusion in the minds and hearts of many Methodists—those, that is, who allow themselves to *ponder* their faith and its problems.

Nowadays however, and almost suddenly, "evangelism" has become a bandwagon "trend"—with all sorts of different groups eager to be aboard. Self-styled evangelicals are speaking up for social action; social activists are claiming that their concerns (and agenda) are evangelistic, too (whoever thought otherwise?). The World Council of Churches has had a "conference" on it (with another planned), we now have the "Lausanne Covenant," The United Methodist Church's Council of Bishops is considering a major declaration on evangelism, and the Roman Catholics have asked that it be included in the agenda of their continuing consultations with the Methodists. I'm as eager and delighted as anybody else about this new enthusiasm and its opening horizons. I even remember an old story of Hal Luccock's, explaining how Catholics and Episcopalians had crosses on their steeples as symbols of their faith in Christ crucified, how Congregationalists had weather vanes up there as tokens of their democratic convictions, whereas Methodists usually had lightning rods, in memory of having once been struck and their fear lest it happen again!

Even so, much of our talk about evangelism remains confused and in need of a careful theological sorting-out. I do not pretend, of course, to be able to do this for The United Methodist Church at large, but I've learned enough from Wesley by now to realize that the issues involved in "offering Christ" to the masses were not at all simple; that he was trying to find and hold to the way between the pitfalls of pietism and antinomianism on one side of the truth and of moralism and works-righteousness on the other side. Unless you're reckless with your words, "evangelical" denotes (and always has denoted) _salvation by faith in Christ crucified_, salvation as the gift of God's unmerited grace, provided freely in and through Christ's suffering love, with no prior moral achievement or merit from the human side. Since the fifth century, "evangelical" has been an antonym to Pelagian moralism in any of its protean forms. But what of the new secular pieties and the new antinomianisms that are now flourishing in our midst?

Most of us know the climactic passage in Tillich's most famous sermon, "You Are Accepted." It has been quoted by Alan Walker in his latest book, which gives it some sort of evangelical _nihil obstat_. And, certainly, it is a valid and eloquent distillate of an essential element in "pure" Lutheran orthodoxy:

> You are accepted. You are accepted, accepted by that which is greater than you. Do not ask for its name now: perhaps you will find it later. Do not try to do anything now; perhaps later you will do much. Do not seek for anything; do not perform anything; do not intend anything. Simply accept the fact that you are accepted.[5]

What is missing here, of course, is any approximation to the Lutheran Christology (there is no mention of Christ anywhere in the sermon). Nor is there any emphasis whatever on those "good works following _after_ faith" that orthodox Lutherans have always stressed. But the instant popularity of this gospel of unconditional acceptance was a sign of that deep relief most moderns feel when anybody offers to cancel all moral conditions for their acceptability either in relation to God or vis-à-vis their fellow human beings. It is heartwarming to think that one is accepted, no matter what; this, of course, is the grain of truth in _I'm O.K., You're O.K._—just as I am, because I am. There is a new egalitarianism in our midst and one bucks a strong tide whenever one wonders aloud about credentials, or standards, or the criteria of one's acceptability (moral, academic, or in any other sphere). Now it is the antinomianism implied in this classical Protestant version of justification as God's acceptance of the sinner in his sin, *no matter what*, that Romans and Anglicans have always feared in the traditional Protestant soteriology, because they see it allowing (yea, encouraging) a pious disregard of moral rules and codes in favor of personal spontaneity in freedom and love (i.e., situation ethics). There is, of course, a world of difference between Luther's doctrine of justification and Tillich's (not their only difference, either, as you may know). Luther faced the manifest scandals of medieval moralism and sacerdotalism and tried to rescue the gospel of God's *unmerited* mercy from their doctrines of merit correlated with their sacerdotal dispensations and disciplines. Tillich had *memories* of a conventional morality of discipline and repression, but he himself had long been liberated from any such traditions by the new amoralisms of the German intelligentsia of the 1920's to which he belonged.[6] Moreover, Luther's stress on Scripture and its Christocentric emphases has no counterpart in Tillich nor the standard Lutheran disjunction between soteriology and culture.

The point to all this for our purposes is that Wesley's heart was strangely warmed "as one was reading *Luther's* preface to the Epistle to the Romans" (May 24, 1738). Later (June 15, 1741), when he finally got around to a more careful reading of Luther's *Commentary on Galatians*, he reacted negatively[7] to what he regarded as its implicit irrationalism and antinomianism. Thus it was that with respect to the relationships between law and gospel and also the specific mode of Christ's redemptive work, Wesley was closer to Calvin than to Luther. But then, after 1765 or thereabouts, under increasing pressure from the "imputationists," Wesley began to pull away from the Calvinists, too, and returned, more and more, to his native holy-living tradition (without, however, abandoning the *sola fide*).[8] From 1770 until his death, the breach with the Calvinists was open and bitter. They never forgave Wesley his synergism; he never dropped his charge that their predestination theories were a charter for antinomianism.

The ruling metaphor of classical Protestant soteriology has always been the courtroom, together with a cluster of forensic concepts about a human offender arraigned before the divine judge who must, if justice is not to be mocked, convict and condemn the offender. What happens then, in the case of the elect, however, is a juridical move in which the judge decides (or has already decided) to commute the sinner's sentence, on the basis of the imputed righteousness of *Christ*. This becomes the *formal* cause of one's justification, whereby the sinner acquires Christ's own perfect righteousness as the just ground for his/her own *acquittal* by God from all condemnation. This is what justification means: to be pardoned, to be regarded and treated as righteous, in and through Christ's saving merit. This forensic imagery has its roots in the Bible (although it is not at all dominant there). It had flourished in feudalism (it is, for example, the presupposition of Anselm's theory of substitutionary atonement[9]). Thereafter, it had been radically transformed in the Reformation, largely by the wiping out of the priestly apparatus that had grown up around it.

There is (we might mention in passing, almost marginally) a very tangled lexical problem here with regard to the biblical terms in which these crucial issues have been defined.[10] The Greek word *dikaioo* belongs to a class of verbs that are formed from adjectives: e.g., *typhlos* =blind; *typhloo*=to blind; *psychros*=cool; *psychroo*=to cool. *Dikaios* means "just"; *dikaioo* means to make just (to strengthen in virtue) or, alternatively, to declare just (as in a court's verdict of acquittal). But this is ambiguous: you can declare a person to be "not guilty" ("just" in that sense) but you cannot *make* a person righteous or "just" by *doing* something to that person. Thus, most Pauline exegetes agree that *dikaioo* is used by St. Paul forensically. And yet when divine action is involved, there must be more than a mere juridical acquittal. "Righteousness" may be *imputed* to a person and he/she may thereby be justified before God, through the merits of Christ. But is nothing like actual righteousness *imparted* at the same time? What is meant by the promise that "if a man is in Christ, he is a new creature . . ."? Does this not imply an actual change of character, along with the change in the God-human relationship? Wesley thought so and was, therefore, committed to a doctrine of justification that involved both a relative and a real change in the forgiven sinner (a relative change in one's forensic status before God and a real change in the moral quality of one's interpersonal relationships).

The official doctrines of the Church of England reflect this forensic tradition (especially in the XXXIX Articles) but Anglicanism had also retained a *therapeutic* emphasis as well: justification as a healing, restorative act, as the turning point in the course of a malignant disease, the beginning of a convalescent process, the goal of which is the complete restoration of the corrupted image of God in man. Justification, then, in Hooker and Taylor and Wesley is both acquittal *and* renewal, imputation *and* impartation, a relative and yet also a real change. In the forensic model of justification, the meaning of 1 Corinthians 5:19 had been reversed, as if St. Paul had said that "God was in Christ reconciling himself to the world . . ." (one can even see this in the Anglican Articles, as in No. II). Wesley did not change this part of the Articles and it still appears in our former Methodist Articles, also No. II. Happily, in Article VIII of the former Evangelical United Brethren "Confession," we find the original Pauline form, "God was in Christ reconciling the world to himself"—which means that, somewhat absent-mindedly, United Methodists have it *both* ways!

By Wesley's time, this older forensic tradition had been generally displaced by what I've been labeling "the gospel of moral rectitude." Thus, he grew up in an Anglican rectory, got his education in an Anglican school and university and then served the Church of England as priest and missionary for more than a decade, with no personal conviction as to salvation by imputation. It is not true, of course, as our typical Methodist hagiography has it, that the young Wesley and his contemporaries (by and large) were mere moralists. When, at the Lord's Table, they prayed (more often than *we* do), "We do not presume to come to this, thy Table trusting in our own righteousness but in thy manifold and great mercy. We are not worthy . . . but thou art the same Lord whose property is always to have mercy," their intentions were as solifidian as any Lutheran's or Calvinist's ever was. But they did insist on a synergism of grace in the sequence of repentance, faith and good works which is why Wesley never repudiated his one great pre-Aldersgate sermon, "The Circumcision of the Heart," with its holy-living theme and its reversed order of placing holiness (in the nascent form of congruent merit) *before* justification. Indeed, he included it in his forty-four "standard sermons"—out of its chronological order!

Even so, it is a fact—it is the *central* fact in the Wesleyan Revival—that from 1738 onwards, Wesley taught the *sola fide* as the first and last article by which the church (and with it the gospel) stands or falls. And yet, he sought a third alternative even here: a fusion of imputation *and* impartation that included both Protestant and Catholic emphases and that brought him reproaches from Anglicans and Calvinists alike. But I have come to believe that it is just this third alternative that has become more and more relevant for ecumenical theology today—especially when all the old forensic images in morality and religion are fading fast or have already lost their decisive influence. Wesley's evangelistic message *combines* radical faith in God's reconciling love in Christ (the inward, personal dimension of salvation) *with* a moral and social agenda implied in and by this love that energizes and guides the Christian life from new birth to maturation, always "in Christ."

We may take two of Wesley's most famous sermons as a summary of this "offering of Christ": (1) "Justification by Faith" (1746)[11] and (2) "The Scripture Way of Salvation" (1765)[12] In "Justification by Faith," there are four questions asked and answered.

Question one: Why and wherefore *justification*? Answer: Sin—and here we have Wesley's doctrine of original sin recapitulated in striking, pungent fashion. Until the sinner is *justified*, his radical unrighteousness leaves him open to a richly deserved unhappiness and damnation.

Question two: What is justification? The answer here is threefold: (a) it is *not* sanctification; (b) it is *not* bare acquittal, least of all an acquittal in which God "believes us righteous when we are unrighteous";[13] (c) it *is* "pardon, the forgiveness of sins."[14]

Question three: "Who are they that are justified?" Answer: The ungodly. Here, however, Wesley turns his own "holy living" tradition around and produces something original. We have seen how that tradition had placed holy intentions ahead of justification. This was the notion that some sort of outward evidence of one's spiritual aspirations ("good works") is prerequisite to actual justification. In 1738, and thereafter, Wesley reversed this order by 180 degrees. "All truly good works *follow* after justification"; justification is, therefore, only for those who have no merit of their own. "Just as I am, without one plea . . ." *is* an authentic evangelical sentiment.

Wesley has a fourth question: On what *terms* may the ungodly be justified? The answer here is *faith*, with no necessary conditions of antecedent obedience of the moral law. And what is faith? It is not only a *belief* in God in Christ (this is mere orthodoxy and the devils are orthodox). It is, rather, "a sure trust and confidence that Christ died for my *sins*, that he loved *me*, and gave himself for me," etc. Faith is the *necessary* condition of justification, and the only *necessary* one (hence "faith alone," *sola fide*). Whatever else we may bring to God, of virtue and holy intentions, repentance and good works, none is a *necessary* condition. Wesley's aim here is to wipe out all possible human pride or complacency in one's salvation and to establish "Jesus [Christ] as the whole and sole propitiation for our sins."

"The Scripture Way of Salvation" is a maturer formulation of Wesley's "offering of Christ," made necessary, in Wesley's judgment, by twenty years of further development in the ferments of the Revival. In this sermon the central questions are reduced to three: What is salvation? What is saving faith? How are we saved *by* faith? Wesley's answers are basically the same as before, but much has been gained in the interim by way of altered nuance, in reaction to misunderstandings among both followers and critics. To begin with, he stresses prevenient grace (which is resistible), and argues that this is a better explanation of the divine initiative than predestination and irresistible grace. He repeats his aphorism that "justification is another word for *pardon*," and then moves on to the controverted issue of the interrelations between justification and sanctification. He denies that these two are different aspects of a single event, and he carefully places sanctification *after* justification, in the ontological order of salvation. They are, however, concurrent in time. When and as we are forgiven, we are also born again, and on the very same terms: i.e., the merits of Christ's atoning love. Thus Wesley can speak of a *relative* change in our status before God (justification), which is all the Moravians and the Puritans would allow in *any* case. But he insists on adding an equal emphasis on the *real* change that takes place in our hearts, lives, and loves—as we become "new creatures in Christ." Thus, he is able to interpret salvation as a *process*: one that begins with justification but that continues thereafter as the regenerate person grows in grace toward sanctification as a flying goal. Justification is what God does *for* us; sanctification is what God does *in* us. In justification we *gain* God's favor; holy living is the life process in which we seek to *retain* it (a distinction that runs back to Philip Melanchthon!). Justification is the *threshold* of faith; sanctification its *fullness*.

This life process is by no means placid nor is its triumphant eventuation ever guaranteed, which is, of course, yet another rejection of any notion of final perseverance. The Christian does not commit *willful* sin. If he does, he loses God's favor and backslides into condemnation. But the impulse and power of sin are not "*destroyed*" in justification or regeneration. They are only "suspended." "Wandering thoughts" (the *fomes peccati* remain, and these must be dealt with in terms of daily repentance, daily renewals of faith, daily exercises of love.

Thus, Wesley understood justification as God's work *for* the repentant sinner, with Christ's mediatorial sacrifice as its sole meritorious cause—to which our only proper response is "acceptance" (i.e., faith). But in the very same transaction there is also a work of divine grace *in* the sinner's heart and moral disposition. Wesley calls this "regeneration" or "new birth," the beginning of the actual restoration of the *imago Dei*, the impartation, by grace, of our "original justice": our

God-given power to love God above all else and all else in God. Justification and regeneration are two aspects of the same mysterious outpouring or inflooding of grace. It is ambiguous and confusing if we blur this distinction between God's action *for* the sinner (reconciliation in love) and God's action *in* the pardoned sinner's heart (restoration of moral responsibility of the human power to avoid or desist from intentional sin). We have no part in our own justification before God, save the passive act of accepting and trusting the merits of Christ. But we do have a crucial part to play in the further business of "growing up into Christ, unto the stature of the perfect man." You can almost always identify a "fundamentalist" theology by noticing, in its preoccupation with soteriology, an indifference to human responsibility in the consequent struggle for God's righteous rule in *all* of human life and society. Conversely, you can find liberalism's cachet in its concern for the Christian's moral and social agenda, with a relative indifference to the fundament on which that agenda rightly rests. The liberal speaks easily of Christ as revealer and exemplar but tends to stammer when pressed back toward any evangelical notions of mediatorial sacrifice. This is why neither fundamentalists nor liberals have a more than tenuous hold on the *full* Christian tradition, as we have seen Wesley trying to put it together and hold it together. Methodists, in his train, have a less than impressive record in doing this as well as he did.

Wesley's first point is that, before and apart from justification, we have only the power to sin even when we "try" not to—and, obviously, we are busy in our exercise of this tragic power. Justification is God's acceptance of just such a sinful person, on account of Christ's merits. Our part in the transaction is a faithful, grateful acceptance of God's acceptance of us. Regeneration is also a work of grace, and with it come the bare beginnings of a restored power to avoid or desist from "known sins." This opens up the possibility of *full* salvation, *full* humanity ("holiness of heart and life"). This gift of restored power not to sin is also the work of grace and all of it is God's sheer, unmerited mercy. We can take no pride in it for ourselves. Our part is gratitude! This is the effect of Christ's ministry of reconciling love—and of a newly active presence of the Holy Spirit in our hearts, leading us toward truth and freedom and love. This creates a new syndrome of relationships (with God, ourselves, and neighbors) and all of it is the fruition of God's grace in Christ and of our response in faith, hope, and love. This response includes the recognition that we live, truly, *in* Christ and *with* Christ, and that the Christian life is a participation with Christ in his mission in the world. This means holy living and holy dying; it means a theology of the Cross *and* a theology of glory. All of this, and more, is thus implied in Wesley's quaint metaphor, "offering Christ."

Nowadays, we are finally beginning to fathom the radical shift that has taken place, and is still taking place, in the moral conscience of moderns. We can see for ourselves (we can see *in* ourselves!) the swift erosion of the old linkage between anxiety and guilt. The level of anxiety remains as high in this society as ever (maybe it is even elevated!). But, everywhere, one notices a shrinkage of any serious sense of damning *guilt before God*. The consequence of this reversal is difficult to grasp but one thing is almost self-evident: viz., the increasing irrelevance of an evangelism that is focused in the old forensic metaphor. It's no big deal nowadays to tell people that their sins are pardoned when they don't really feel *guilty* (at least not in the traditional sense), but only anxious, victimized, and put upon. Increasingly, it is not much more than "ho-hum" to proclaim that "you are accepted" to people who have already been told that they ought to have *been* accepted, by rights, *long since*. Christian evangelists must now realize that they have to find a true word of gospel for "the guiltless," those who are no longer contrite but are still nonetheless hopeless. We must seek and find a new version of the old gospel of grace and hope through Christ in the Spirit. As Richard Niebuhr might remind us, it is no gospel at all anymore (even if it ever was), to speak of "a God without wrath who brought men without sin into a kingdom without judgment through the ministrations of a Christ without a Cross."[15]

For if it is true that those who *feel* guiltless no longer need a gospel of forensic acquittal, it is also true that those who *are* hopeless need something a good deal better than "peak experiences" or extended episodes of "expanded consciousness." What kind of a gospel is it that extols freedom and happiness within the ironic brackets of transience and death? What is there to hope for if my highest aspirations are never to come to any full fruition? Are life's agonies and ecstasies really worth it after all?

Suppose we let the forensic metaphors go (as I think we may) and turn, as so many have, to therapeutic metaphors, as in the pastoral counseling movement, generally. It must be stressed that this is a definite advance, to be both welcomed and also incorporated into our theology, ethics, and so forth. But it should be obvious that *therapy*, in all of its images, connotes *amelioration* and not full self-realization of "salvation." Suppose a given therapy is *relatively* successful (which, of course, is the only way one can speak of therapy). Suppose a neurotic's repressed psychic energies are freed up and made newly available for self-expression. Suppose oppressed groups are liberated, as surely they ought to and must be. What then? Therapy or liberation or whatever are never ends in themselves. They are *means*. But means to *what end*, except lasting human joy and happiness? And what is our assurance that these ends can be attained by these means?

Beyond the courtroom and the clinic, therefore, the human hunger for happiness reaches out toward some sovereign power that really cares and is truly sovereign, that is more than a bloodless ideal or a human aspiration that is finally mocked by transience and death. The good news we really need to hear is that "*God* so loved the world that he gave of himself to the world in order that that world [and we] might not perish [in final meaninglessness] but have eternal life [the full human potential, here and hereafter]." There's nothing forensic in this old verse and it reaches far beyond any of the current accounts I know about "peak experiences," *satori*, "cosmic consciousness," and the like. The Christian gospel is the message of God's suffering, redemptive, reconciling love that initiates a new life in Christ within the body of Christ. "You who are justified by faith" (as St. Paul puts it) "are in Christ Jesus, by God's own act, for God has made him our wisdom and our righteousness [justification]; in him we are consecrated and set free" [liberated!].[16] Those for whom this is a living faith have a different ground for hope than ever they could have otherwise.

I have cited only two of the great gospel promises, two out of at least a hundred, which point to the mystery of salvation beyond any earthly self-salvation or any heavenly courtroom. They speak of a theonomous transaction, the essence of which is reconciliation between unhappy sinners and the holy God, which alters *all* the meanings of human life and death. On the human side, there are two conditions: repentance and faith. But the divine agent in the transaction is Jesus Christ, without whose redemptive love we would not have the reality of God's grace suffusing and hallowing the whole of life. It is in Christ that we find our true fulfillment in this life "and in the life of the world to come."

Human life *must* be lived in and by grace or else it will be lived gracelessly and ungraciously and death will find us not only vulnerable but literally hopeless. Autonomous humanity is foredoomed to hollow triumphs—to aspirations forever thwarted, to victories that wreak havoc and that leave the victors still unfulfilled. The gospel is

God's enacted promise in Christ that we can live intentionally, follow-ing the inner leadings of the Holy Spirit, obedient to what we are given to know of God's will, growing ever into a deeper faith and a truer happiness than we could ever know, in and for and by ourselves. And Jesus Christ is the guarantor and agent of this promise, both in revealing God's love (in our human lot and all its tragedy), and in renewing our hope, in, through, and beyond tragedy. His power, shared with us, is the victory over sin and death, i.e., over their power to cor-rupt our faith, hope, and love. He is the enacted promise that since we *are* God's children, we can anticipate our future. Its details are shroud-ed; we must wait and work in faith and hope, but this much we can count on now (and in any case): "that when he shall appear, we shall be like him, and shall see him (and ourselves) as he really is (and our-selves as he meant us to become)."[17]

The Christian gospel for the guiltless is rather less that he has appeased the Father's wrath than that he is the agent of the Father's redemptive compassion. This is not at all to reject the still living truth in the grand article of justification. It is only to stress, more than our older Protestant traditions did, the theme of salvation by *participation*— in God's love in Christ through the Spirit. Our real hope lies in God's grace and in his purpose to restore such overreachers as we are to that happiness wherein human outreach (within its proper frame of depen-dence, trust, and obedience) does in fact achieve the happiness that God intends for his children—for *all* his children.

The gospel call is still the same: "Repent and believe the Gospel"—the good news that God is indeed the giver of life's mean-ings and joys and hopes, that life in his love is ultimately secure and can even now be serene, since all its final meanings (in life *and* death) are in his hands. This is the good news: that "God is on *our* side" (Rom. 8:31). What then can separate us from the love of Christ, save unfaith or (what amounts to the same thing) self-righteousness?

In *these* terms, or something like them, the gospel is still alive and well and was never more desperately needed than by those guiltless souls whose guiltlessness has added to their final hopelessness. *Repent* (let the Holy Spirit teach you the real truth about your sin, your need, your potential)! *Believe* the gospel, accept your radical dependence upon God's freely offered gifts of love and joy. *Go on toward holiness* (the per-fect love of God and neighbor) and *expect* to be made perfect in love in this life. In such a faith and hope as this we might then look *within* with new and grace-filled insights as to God's provisions for *self*-acceptance and *self*-affirmation. We might, even at the same time, look *outward*, toward all those tasks that are prompted by human need and the imperatives of sacrificial love. And we really would be "new creatures." The old self-stultifications of life would have begun to "pass away." Can you suggest a much better definition than this of the Christian life—or, what amounts to the same thing, of *human life at its best?*

IV: "Holiness of Heart and Life"

ost non-Methodists, and not a few Methodists, would be startled by some of the questions a Methodist ordinand is asked in the course of his "being received into full connection" (i.e., membership) in an Annual Conference. The present list[1] is a curious conflation of various examinations that Wesley devised for "admitting" his own preachers into "connection."[2] When one recalls that these men were all laymen, it is obvious that these queries are also applicable, in principle, to any and all baptized/confirmed Christians. Their being reserved now for ordinands does not alter the fact that, for Wesley, they were appropriate clues for the examination (*self*-examination!) of all earnest Christians, to be asked and answered with unflinching seriousness.

The first one is commonplace enough. But then come three real "stickers," certainly for sensitive and knowledgeable young men and women nowadays—and for the generality of Christians of any age and station:

1. *Have you faith in Christ?*
2. *Are you going on to perfection?*
3. *Do you expect to be made perfect in love in this life?*[3]
4. *Are you earnestly striving after it?*[4]

The requisite answer, in each case, is affirmative!

All too often, in actual current circumstances (as Methodists will know from experience), these probes into the very heart of a person's Christian self-understanding are dealt with in a way that appeals to the individual interpretation of the several ordinands, few of whom have puzzled their way deeply enough into the Wesleyan doctrine of perfection to have clear and responsible commitments to what they are professing ritually. Nor is it always and altogether clear to their elders in the Conference!

There are at least two reasons for this pious confusion. The first, of course, is a widespread consensus in modern culture (instructed as we have been by depth psychology, together with an inbred cynicism) that rejects any notion of "perfection" simply out of hand and would, therefore, assess anybody's serious expectation of being "made perfect in love *in this life*" as symptomatic of a psychotic delusion. The second reason is historical and is related to the greatest tragedy in Methodist history: the nineteenth century conflicts that swirled around Wesley's emphasis upon "holiness of heart and life" and its alterations and distortions at the hands of men and women who were seeking to be faithful Wesleyans (on both sides!) without having experienced anything close to the theological and spiritual struggles out of which his own original synthesis had emerged. The ironic outcome of this process (especially in America) was that the keystone in the arch of Wesley's own theological "system" came to be a pebble in the shoes of standard-brand Methodists, even as a distorted version of Wesley's doctrine of sanctification (as "a second and separate work of grace *subsequent* to regeneration") was becoming a shibboleth of self-righteousness amongst a pious minority of Methodists who professed themselves holier than the rest. That conflict and its abrasions had the effect of leaving the average Methodist (and many much above that average) alienated even by the bare terms—"holiness," "Christian perfection," "sanctification"—not to speak of an aversion toward those persons who actually profess such spiritual attainments.

There's this occasional fantasy that sometimes crops up in my daydreaming: to set some of our curial "experts" onto a "scientific study in depth"—replete with questionnaires, computers, the whole apparatus of apparent objectivity! Their project would be to analyze a whole series of different groups in The United Methodist Church by double-blinding them on these three questions about "perfection in this life" and then assessing their responses! For example: it is the bishop who asks these questions, but how many bishops still "expect to be made perfect in love in this life"? How many other Methodists expect how many bishops (and which bishops) so to be perfected? The computer would be programmed to activate a rocket for every one who claimed he already was! This would only be for starters. How many bureaucrats or journalists "are earnestly seeking after perfection"?—and how many correlations could be delineated between, say, staff people in "global ministries," "church and society," "discipleship" or wherever? How many professors and in what disciplines? How many pastors (correlated with which seminaries, and when)? How many layfolk—categorized according to age, sex, race, jurisdictions, etc., etc.? This would not be nearly as dubious and fruitless as many another solemn study project on which we have already expended unreasonable sums of money and personnel.

But I always awake from such fantasizing with a sad, grim smile—since I know as well as you that any results from this sort of thing would be doubly misleading. On the one hand, there are Methodists whom I know who are already nearer to what Wesley would have recognized as "perfection" than *they* are aware of, or would ever admit to. And, on the other hand, there are many "professors of true holiness" who come across as proud of being holier than the rest of us—and this helps to reinforce the phobias that standard-brand Methodists already have, in line with their inbred negative stereotypes. Thus, by a series of multiple ironies, the Methodists have been deprived of a vital element in their heritage and have been spiritually impoverished as a result (on *both* sides). Our traditional emphasis on "the spiritual life" is more ambiguous than it should be and our traditional commitments to social reform are less effectual. And it goes without saying that *non*-Methodists are, for the most part, baffled or unedified by this disintegration of a great tradition.

This is why the task of commenting on the theme of "holiness of heart and life" to an audience of contemporary Christians gives one the uneasy feeling that he/she *begins* by being overexposed to misunderstanding. My situation here reminds me of one of the apocryphal stories that abound in Rome about Pope John XXIII—this one before he was pope (actually when he was papal nuncio in Paris). At a banquet there for the diplomatic corps, Msgr. Roncalli was seated next to a buxom lady whose stylish gown had been designed by a minimalist (or maximalist, depending on one's viewpoint). When the fruit course was served, she declined; whereupon Msgr. Roncalli urged her to try an apple, explaining, when asked why, that it was an apple that had helped Eve to realize *her* condition!

But I take comfort and courage in such a venture from the undeniable fact that John Wesley believed and taught an explicit doctrine of "holiness" as the goal and crown of the Christian life, and if this gives you trouble, the burden of proof shifts over onto your side (if, that is, you profess to be a Wesleyan at all) to explain why you are prepared to reject or ignore what he regarded as not only essential but climactic. His irreducible minimum of Christian fundamentals were, as we have seen, three: (1) sin and repentance (i.e., self-knowledge), (2) justification and pardon (i.e., assurance) and (3) "holiness of heart and life."[5] "Sanctification," "perfect love," "Christian perfection" were various synonyms, in his vocabulary, for "holiness," and he rang the changes on this theme throughout his whole evangelistic career, insisting that it was the special mission of the Methodists to hold "and to spread [this doctrine of] scriptural holiness over the land."[6]

It is important, therefore, always to start with Wesley's first conversion (1725), a conversion to the ideal of holy living, and to remember that he never thereafter abandoned this ideal even when further conversions (and other experiences) complicated his interpretation of it by a good deal.[7] The seed of the idea had been planted in his mind in the Epworth parsonage by Susanna, one of whose favorite devotional texts was Lorenzo Scupoli's (or, as was then thought, Juan de Castaniza's) *Spiritual Struggle*.[8] The seed had flowered under the stimulus of Jeremy Taylor, Thomas à Kempis, William Law and others. But the idea of perfection as a dynamic *process* with a flying goal did not take its mature form until, finally, Wesley found his way back to the great devotional traditions of Eastern Orthodoxy—Clement of Alexandria, Gregory of Nyssa, Macarius of Egypt, and others.[9] The first fruits of these discoveries may be seen in the only great sermon of his of which we have any record before 1738. This was "The Circumcision of the Heart" (written in December of 1732 and preached in St. Mary's on January 1, 1733 [which was not New Year's Day on the then current calendar]). Too little attention has been paid to the implications of the fact that Wesley never discarded this sermon or even recast it. It turns up, in its original text but out of its chronological order, as No. XIII in *Sermons on Several Occasions*, Vol. II, 1748.[10]

It is true, that in those years, 1725-38, he consistently misplaced "holiness" (or pure intentions) *before* justification, as preparatory to it. Bishop George Bull and most other Anglicans from Bull to Tillotson had done the same thing—and Wesley would berate them for it later on. One of the decisive shifts in his 1738 transformation was the reversal of this order. Thereafter, justification always stands first, without any antecedent "holiness" or merit of any kind as a *necessary* precondition to human salvation. Our natural sinful state can be dealt with only by God's sheer gratuitous mercy, based upon Christ's freely offered mediatorial merit. Then, and only then, can anything like new birth and Christian nurture *begin* to restore the power not to sin intentionally which may then be developed further in a nurturing process toward the goal of sanctification: "the mature man in Christ." This relation of justification to sanctification was the critical issue that had first been raised for Wesley in his encounters with the Herrnhuters and Salzburgers in Georgia. It was the main issue that divided Wesley and Whitefield almost as soon as the Revival began. It was the issue on which Wesley and Count von Zinzendorf soon clashed and finally parted.

It is easy for us to miss the originality of this Wesleyan view of faith alone and holy living *held together*. Here was a great evangelist preaching up *sola fide* and, at the very same time, teaching his converts to go on to perfection and to expect it *in this life*! His critics were quick to notice this strange move and to seize upon it as proof of Wesley's inconsistency.[11] Actually, it was yet another of Wesley's characteristic "third alternatives"—maybe his most original one. In this view, the stages of the unfolding Christian life may be laid out in something like the following sequence (a psychological sequence which was more nearly concurrent than spaced out): (1) contrition and repentance (true self-knowledge); (2) justification by faith alone (with Christ's atonement as the *meritorious* but not the *formal* cause for, remember, this was the crux of his quarrel with the Calvinists!);[12] (3) regeneration ("new birth") issuing in (4) Christian nurture in intensive small encounter groups (with no carpets and no nonsense!); looking toward (5) maturation into "holiness," always in its twin dimensions ("internal holiness" [our *love of God* and neighbor] and "external holiness" [our *love of God and of neighbor*!]). All this was aimed at a climax (6) "perfect love" of God and neighbor as the Spirit's greatest *gift* (which means that, in Wesley's mind, sanctification *by faith alone* was as self-evident as justification ever was, never a moral achievement). And yet, as Wesley never ceased to insist, none of these "stages" is static, none of them so fully completed that one may not lapse from it by unbelief or willful sin—hence his rejection of "final perseverance." What mattered most was that "going on to perfection" has a consistent character and a clear end in view: (1) *love* (of God and neighbor), (2) *trust* (in Christ and the sufficiency of his grace) and (3) *joy* (joy upwelling in the heart from the "prevenience" of the indwelling Spirit). This *is* "holy living": to love God and neighbor with all your heart, to trust securely in Christ's merits, and to live joyously "in the Spirit"!

But this vital linkage between faith alone and holy living was forever being misconstrued and Wesley was forever being baffled by its misconstructions. Somehow, he could never grasp the fact that people formed by the traditions of Latin Christianity were bound to understand "perfection" as *perfectus* (*perfected*)—i.e., as a finished state of completed growth, *ne plus ultra*! For him, certainly since his own discoveries of the early fathers, "perfection" meant "perfecting" (*teleiosis*), with further horizons of love and of participation in God always opening up *beyond* any given level of spiritual progress. This seemed so *obvious* to him that he allowed himself a swig of smug triumphalism:

> *It has been frequently observed, that [in the Reformation time] very few were clear in their judgment both with regard to justification and sanctification. Many who have spoken and written admirably well concerning justification had no clear conception, nay, were totally ignorant of the doctrine of sanctification. Who has wrote more ably than Martin Luther on justification by faith alone? And who was more ignorant of the doctrine of sanctification, or more confused in his conceptions of it? . . . On the other hand, how many writers of the Romish Church (as Francis Sales and Juan de Castaniza) have wrote strongly and scripturally on sanctification, who, nevertheless, were entirely unacquainted with the nature of justification! insomuch that the whole body of their Divines at the Council of Trent totally confound sanctification and justification together. But it has pleased God to give the Methodists a full and clear knowledge of each, and the wide difference between them.* 13

Regeneration ("new birth," "change of heart") is a concurrent effect alongside justification.[14] The sense of God's unmerited favor prompts an inner transformation, a new disposition toward God and neighbor, a new *self*-understanding, a new outlook and hope. Even so, "this is only the threshold of sanctification...." The Christian life goes on from here, in a dynamic process of nurture, piety, activity—and of *expectation*: that what is imputed in justification will be *imparted* in the Christian life and its fulfillment. *This* is "Christian perfection"—"to be made perfect in love in this life," even if only in the hour of death (which was Wesley's normal "calendar" for it).

>   *It is, then, a great blessing given to this people, that as*
> *they do not think or speak of justification so as to supersede*
> *sanctification, so neither do they think or speak of sanctifica-*
> *tion so as to supersede justification. They take care to keep*
> *each in its own place, laying equal stress on one and the*
> *other. They know God has joined these together, and it is not*
> *for man to put down asunder. Therefore, they maintain, with*
> *equal zeal and diligence, the doctrine of free, full, present jus-*
> *tification, on the one hand, and of entire sanctification both*
> *of heart and life, on the other; being as tenacious of inward*
> *holiness as any mystic, and of outward [holiness] as any*
> *Pharisee.*
>
>   *Who then is a Christian, according to the light which*
> *God hath vouchsafed to this [Methodist] people? He that,*
> *being "justified by faith, hath peace with God through our*
> *Lord Jesus Christ," and, at the same time, is "born again,"*
> *"born from above," "born of the Spirit"; inwardly changed*
> *from the image of the devil, to that "image of God wherein*
> *he was created"; he that finds the love of God shed abroad*
> *in his heart by the Holy Ghost which is given unto him,*
> *and whom this love sweetly constrains to love his neighbor*
> *(i.e., every man) as himself; he that has learned of his Lord*
> *to be meek and lowly in heart, and in every state to be con-*
> *tent; he in whom is that whole mind, all those tempers,*
> *which are also in Christ Jesus; he that abstains from all*
> *appearance of evil in his actions, and that offends not with*
> *his tongue; he that walks in all the commandments of God,*
> *and in all his ordinances, blameless; he that, in all his inter-*
> *course with men, does to others as he would they should do*
> *to him; and in his whole life and conversation, whether he*
> *eats or drinks, or whatsoever he doeth, doeth all to the glory*
> *of God.*[15]

This is an important version of Wesley's doctrine of "holiness of heart and life" in his own words. Its development (apart from *this* statement) is marked out in a series of six landmark sermons over the six-decade span of his ministry. (1) "The Circumcision of the Heart" which, as we have already seen, was his first full definition of the holy living tradition. (2) "Christian Perfection" is a sermonic essay never preached, but published first in 1741 with the express encouragement of Bishop Edmund Gibson of London—who could tell an authentic version of the holy living motif when he saw one. (3) "Sin in Believers" is something of an afterthought, added (in 1763) to correct mistaken interpretations of "Christian Perfection," as if it implied *sinless* perfection. It doesn't, and never did, for Wesley. (4) "The Lord Our Righteousness" (1765) marks the decisive parting of the ways between Wesley and the Calvinists—which is to say, a majority of the evangelicals in the Church of England and most Nonconformists, too. The issue, as we have seen, is between "formal cause" and "meritorious cause." This may sound like a quibble until you probe it more closely (like reading the debates at Trent[16] and Bellarmine[17] and Davenant![18]). Actually, it's the same issue as between imputation and impartation, between predestination and prevenience. "Formal cause" (to the Calvinists) implied predestination; "meritorious cause" implied God's prevenience and human synergism. The first is "protestant," the second is "catholic." And Wesley, after a full generation of evangelical preaching of justification, continues to insist that Christ's death is the *meritorious* cause of our justification but not the *formal* cause (which he takes to be God's primordial covenant that those who believe shall be saved and those who refuse shall not).

Sermon No. 5 would have to be "On Working Out Our Own Salvation" (1785), a remarkable statement of Wesley's "synergism" and, maybe, his most carefully nuanced exposition of "faith alone" and "holy living."[19] Our last sermon (6), and a fitting climax for the series, is also the last sermon published in Wesley's lifetime. Its theme is "The Wedding Garment." I had never realized until recently (after all these years of poking around, too) that this particular parable had been a sort of shibboleth between the partisans of *sola fide* and of "holy living." What *does* "the wedding garment" signify? To the Calvinists it meant the spotless robe of Christ's righteousness flung as a cover over the "filthy rags" of our *un*righteousness. To the Anglicans generally it had signified holiness itself—i.e., that Christian moral character that is attained by God's *gift* of grace and his *demand* for holy living. With death only months away, Wesley restates his basic conviction, first fixed in 1725: that "the wedding garment signifies holiness, neither more nor less"—the holiness specified in Hebrews 12:14, "without which no man shall see the Lord." Have you ever preached on this parable or heard it preached on? Have you ever considered how much this issue matters to us *today?*

Holiness as a vision of the human potential is an easily distorted notion, and you can see Wesley struggling with its misunderstandings in his *Plain Account of Christian Perfection as Believed and Taught by the Rev. Mr. John Wesley from the Year 1725 to 1765* and thereafter (six editions from 1766 to 1789). There is also that wonderful little pamphlet of 1762 entitled *Cautions and Directions Given to the Greatest Professors in the Methodist Societies*,[20] where the "professors" (i.e., of perfection) are given six highly relevant advices: (1) against pride and self-righteousness; (2) against pride's daughter, *enthusiasm* (defined as grasping for happiness without submitting oneself to its necessary preconditions); (3) against *antinomianism* (doing your own thing, regardless); (4) against sins of *omission* (getting tired and supposing that what you've already done is plenty—or at least enough); (5) against desiring anything above God, and (6) against *schism* (which, as Wesley saw it,[21] was something like pious cantankerousness!). Obviously, these "cautions and directions" were timely—prompted by more than a few rare cases of self-righteousness and spiritual elitism. Indeed, it was just this syndrome of self-righteousness amongst the holiness people that led "mainstream" Methodists finally to throw the Wesleyan baby of true holiness out with the "second blessing" bath water!

Now I don't have to tell you that, nowadays, we're in another valley of decision. New versions of "holiness," "pentecostalism," "enthusiasm," charismatic renewal, and spiritual elitism are abroad in the land, spreading the usual confusion and acrimony that seem to come along with religious revivals generally. Many United Methodist Church leaders (bishops, cathedral preachers, bureaucrats)—and leaders in other churches, too—are reacting very much like the Anglican hierarchy reacted to the Methodists in the eighteenth century. There *are* hyperpituitary Christians in our midst and they *are* divisive. But then, so also were the early Methodists! There *are* vast numbers of nominal Christians amongst us, and they are depressing. So, why should I be upset when a tongue-speaker or a Jesus freak tells me, in a patronizing tone, that I'm unsaved, or that he is holier-than-I (as several have)? Well, for one thing and obviously, my own spiritual pride and personal vanity are offended (which means, alas, that he's partially right!).

But the real tragedy is that most of us have never grasped Wesley's crucial distinction between the *extraordinary* gifts of the Spirit (healing, tongues, prophecy, discernment of spirits, teaching, and the like) and the *ordinary* fruits of the Spirit which norm everything in the Christian life, including the extraordinary gifts of the Spirit ("love, joy, peace, patience, kindness, goodness, fidelity, gentleness, and self-control"[22]).

There are many people in the world whose *extraordinary* gifts of the Spirit surpass my own by a great deal, and I ought always to *rejoice* in their talents. Even so, I have the right and duty to pass judgment on them—not in terms of their "gifts" but rather their "fruits"—and they must be willing to have their gifts so judged, by the "ordinary" Christian virtues that are normative for all converted Christians. The moment one is impatient with or censorious about another's spiritual progress—or unkind, ungentle, etc., from either side (pietists denouncing the activists, activists scorning pietists, and all that!)—in *that* moment, even holy folk have backslidden into substandard Christianity, whatever their professions or rhetoric may be. Let *me* learn to rejoice in all extraordinary gifts; let *them* learn to repent of any spiritual pride they may discover in their hearts. Let us both cultivate the ordinary fruits of the Spirit and enjoy them wherever found. "If their *hearts* be as our *hearts*, let us join hands"; *this*, of course, is what Wesley meant by "catholic spirit."[23] If The United Methodist Church cannot provide as welcome a home for her right-wing Montanists as she has for her left-wing "prophets," she will have proved herself less catholic than Wesley—or St. Paul ever supposed a church should be and still deserve the name "church" (versus a "sect").

We know (or our liberal forefathers knew) the distortions of the Wesleyan doctrine of holiness that led to its disrepute and abandonment. Wesley himself did not use the phrase, "sinless perfection"—with its simplistic view of the power not to sin—but he did not guard himself against it as carefully as he might have. And so it turned up, in the Methodist holiness movement, as a shift from a notion of perfecting (or perfectible) perfection over to a claim of perfected perfection. Then came a very dubious distinction, still insisted on in holiness circles, between "a perfect heart" and "a perfect character." For example, in the current *Manual* of the Church of the Nazarene (p. 52, par. 36) such a distinction is emphasized: "The perfect heart is obtained in an instant, the result of entire sanctification, but a perfect character is the result of growth in grace." Closer home, it is fairly clear (to me, at least) that Article XI in par. 69 of the former Evangelical United Brethren Confession is closer to the nineteenth century pietist distortions of the doctrine of sanctification than to Wesley's own version of the doctrine. Either way, we have problems, *and* a signal ecumenical opportunity!

Now, I'm not about to claim to be the first man since Wesley to understand what he meant by "holiness of heart and life"—Lindstrom, Flew, Sangster, and others have probed this doctrine in considerable depth. But the fact is that modern American Methodists have relegated the whole business to the margin of their interests, as if holiness were just another of Wesley's eighteenth century crotchets, like his belief in ghosts and witchcraft. This seems to me all the more tragic because, after all my days and nights of sitting up with this strange man—hearing him and asking him questions—I've come to believe that he's *got* something that all of us need, a view that is as contemporary as transactional analysis (and much more realistic), a doctrine that is truly ecumenical: "catholic, evangelical *and* reformed." This vision of the Christian life (complex in many ways, yet quite simple at its core) might help us toward that renewal of the church that we keep talking about and praying for and are yet denied because of our partisan confusions.

What seems obvious to everyone is that Wesley was obsessed with ideas about Christian discipline and duty. His wide assortment of "rules," together with his incessant exhortations to Christian morality all combine to give us a picture of the prototypical Methodist moralist and legalist that we all know too well and have become ourselves, all too often: a church whose coat-of-arms might very well have on it a General Conference resolution rampant, over a local congregation dormant, with a Latin motto on the scroll, *Possumus non peccare* (we can stop sinning [and stop *other* people from sinning!] if only we try hard enough!). In any case, it does seem obvious that Wesley must have been a deontologist in ethics—forever asking about the *ought* in moral issues, about one's *duty* or about the rules for authentic Christian living. Now, it is generally agreed, in the history of ethics and moral theory, that deontology and Christian perfection do not mix readily. Take Kant (Wesley's younger contemporary) who was so certain that the "ought" and the "is" do not coincide in this life—ever—that, rationalist as he was, he concluded that there really must be a *heavenly* life—where duty and happiness *do* coexist, as they *ought to*.

But take a closer look at Wesley and a surprising fact emerges (at least it surprised me when I first realized what I was seeing, after all these years!). This man was a *eudaemonist*, convinced and consistent all his life. All his emphases on duty and discipline are auxiliary to his main concern for human *happiness* (blessedness, etc.). He believed (with Aquinas, Erasmus, and Richard Lucas[24] before him) that all our truly human aspirations are oriented toward *happiness*. "The best end which any creature can pursue is happiness in God."[25] The human tragedy, therefore, is that persons seek happiness (as they *must*) but in false values that leave them unhappy, in earthly quests that leave them frustrated if unattained or unsatisfied even when attained. Wesley uses a wealth of illustrations and allusions to make this crucial point over and over again—that only misery follows false loves and false values. The world is awash with unhappiness, but always this is the effect of misplaced affections, misconceived goals, the tragic futility of self-love curving back upon itself.

In a hundred different ways, Wesley repeats the thesis: human unhappiness, in any and all its forms, comes from setting our love of creation above our love of the Creator, our love of self above our love of neighbor. But this is the generic definition of *unholiness*: innocent love corrupted by false loves. Thus he can argue that only the holy are truly happy, only the hallowed life is truly blessed, only the truly loving are actually joyful. The human potential is not self-fulfilling—and in any case it is bracketed by transience and death. All our truly human aspirations are self-transcending: they point to the love of God and neighbor as their true norms. But this is the essence of *holiness. Inward* holiness is, preeminently, our love of God, the love of God above all else and all else in God. *Outward* holiness is our consequent love of neighbor (*all* God's children, every accessible human being whom we may serve) with a love that springs from our love of God and that seeks the neighbor's well-being as the precondition of our own proper self-love. There's a lot of loose talk nowadays about having to love ourselves in order to be able to love others (as if this were a proper exegesis of "love your neighbor as yourself"). There *is* a grain of vital truth here: self-loathing on whatever account corrupts all our relations with all others. But there's a greater danger—and one can see it in the mounting tide of narcissism in pop-psychotherapy and in the rising vogue for public ego-trips in our pop-culture. For me to have to love myself self-consciously in order to be able to love you unself-consciously is likely to deceive us both: it gets the ends and means of our moral intentions confused. "Inward" and "outward" holiness must be integrated, into a true "whole-i-ness."

In Wesley's case, the patterns of interrelationship are plain. In half a hundred places he sums up *"holy living," "holiness," "sanctification," "Christian perfection"* in words like these:

> What is religion then? It is easy to answer, if we con-
> sult the oracles of God. Accounting to these, it lies in one
> single point: it is neither more nor less than love. It is the
> love which "is the fulfilling of the law, the end of the com-

mandment." Religion is the love of God and our neigh-
bour; that is, every man under heaven. [26]

And this is happiness and joy, as well, the truest and most enduring joy
we ever know. We have fifty-four quotes where Wesley explicitly pairs
off "happy and holy" (or vice versa) and the correlation is constant
throughout his works and his career. [27]

It's odd, isn't it, that for so many of us, terms like "holy" and "sanctified" sound so otherworldly, and yet we can talk about "happy" and
"unhappy" with no embarrassment whatever? If I asked you if you
were happy, your answer might be "yes," "no," or "somewhat," but at
least you'd understand my concern. But, if I asked you how "holy" you
were, you'd think I'd looped. And yet, would it be impertinent, really,
for me to ask you if you do love God preeminently, as far as you are
aware of your own best intentions? If you were willing to answer at all,
then any answer you gave would reflect your ideas about "inward"
holiness in Wesley's sense. And if I then could ask, "Do you love all your
fellow human beings individually and collectively—i.e., are you intel-
ligently and actively concerned for *their* well-being as far as your intentions and resources and actions are concerned?"—then any answer you
gave here would expose your ideas of "outward" holiness! The sum of
both answers would give us both a reliable reading as to your concept
and your experience of *true happiness.*

To love God is not merely a friendly feeling toward the ground of
being, nor a mood of prayer and piety toward "The Man Upstairs." It
is, rather, an awareness of our radical dependence upon God's grace
and our gladness that this is the truth about our lives. It means a sense
of Holy Presence and of security and warmth in that Presence. It
means our recognition of God's upholding love and our gratitude for
his love. It means serenity in the face of death because of our confidence that God's love cannot be conquered or canceled by death. And,
most of all, it means having no other gods of our own, since the *first*
commandment is also the last!

But overreaching humans cannot "obey" the command to love
God as simple acts of choice or even as a life program aimed at self-
salvation and happiness. This is why there's so much confusion nowadays about all these self-help programs, mystical exaltations ("religious
highs" and things like that), as if this sort of thing could ever be equat-
ed with authentic Christian faith and love. This is why holy living is
not, strictly speaking, a human achievement or any part of sinful

humanity's "natural capacity" to initiate. It is not, at bottom, part of the human potential, save in the carefully guarded sense that God's prevenient grace stimulates and enables us to respond, positively and gratefully. "We love *him* because he first loved *us*." It is God's *initiative* that makes possible our *response*; it is his *self*-presentation in Christ that frees us to accept his acceptance of us. It is his saving work in our justification that liberates us for valid ethical endeavor: in our personal maturations in grace and in our involvements in all effective transformations of society under the aegis of the Kingdom of God.

Thus "faith alone" remains as the threshold of all true holiness in heart and life—and of human happiness— here and hereafter. Wesley analyzes this in a remarkable trio of sermons on "The Law Established Through Faith."[28] Faith stands first (*sola fide*) but not as an end in itself. Nor is it a meritorious *act*, as many fundamentalists seem to insist. Rather, faith is a means in order to *love* just as love is in order to *goodness*, just as goodness is in order to *happiness*—which is what God made us for, in this world—and the next. *This* is "holy living."

Likewise, our love of neighbor (if it ever becomes more than benevolent feeling) follows from our love of God. Love of neighbor is a function of our concern to hallow *all* of life, in all of its occasions, great and small. It is our part in answering the Lord's prayer, "Thy Kingdom come, thy will *be done on earth* . . . " [Why *can't* we ever get that punctuation right? The comma belongs after "*on earth*," not before!]. In any case, I'd feel easier with my pietist friends if their neighborly love were not so self-selective of their own kind. I'd feel easier about my activist colleagues if their neighborly love weren't so often ruthless. The only love I've ever known that I've trusted and felt sustained by was *from* God, *through* men and women whose love was unselfish—i.e., people who have loved me grace-fully. This indeed is what I *mean* by love—and all of us have been blessed by it, most of us far beyond our deservings or gratitude. It is grace-filled love that helps us become human and that nourishes our humanity.

This is why there was so much *joy* in Wesley (and in the best Wesleyan traditions of holiness of heart and life)—so much happiness in a man who had been taught from infancy to hold his emotions in check and whose temperament was remarkably cool (even amidst the violent emotions he managed to stir up). He was not an exuberant type and he deplored all flippancy and small talk. This is one reason why he has been easier for me to study than he would have been to live and work with. And yet, there *is* this strange, insistent reality of cheerfulness and high spirits that keeps breaking through his knit-browed earnestness. He was, I've come finally to realize, a happy man, in his own sense of "happiness": the human affects of loving God and serving others. And this joyousness of his (and of his brother Charles even more) was infectious. It became a part of the Methodist tradition, its hymnody, its distinctive lifestyle. Some of it still continues in our current tradition—sometimes trivialized, often faked. But what a wonder it would be if we could recover such a tradition's inner springs: viz., the grace of our Lord Jesus Christ who is the Father's redemptive love making life holy and happy, in and by the power of the Holy Spirit in our hearts! *Then*, we'd have no more trouble with those questions about going on to perfection, etc.! *Are* you? Yes, by God's grace! Then, right on! Praise the Lord!

Wesley died happy—singing and praying. The particular hymn that came to him on that last day was already a favorite with all those people in that little room in the house on City Road. It was by Isaac Watts—a sort of poetic comment on the "art of holy *dying*" that Wesley had so long taught his people as the converse of "the art of holy *living*." "I'll praise my Maker while I've breath. . . ." What we can see now, I hope, is that this was a reiteration, *in extremis*, of what Wesley had always said the breath of life is for—and what it had been for, for him, throughout his whole incredible career. God *has* made us for himself. Our first and last end *is* to love him, and to *enjoy him* forever. This *is* holiness of heart and life, and it was Wesley's witness in life *and* death. It was, therefore, a last reprise of the theme of that first conversion, long ago:

> *I'll praise my Maker while I've breath*
> *And, when my voice is lost in death,*
> *Praise shall employ my nobler powers.*
> *My days of praise shall ne'er be past,*
> *While life and thought and being last,*
> *And immortality endures.*
> *Amen!*

Notes

I: "Plundering the Egyptians"

1. "The Denman Lectures on Evangelism," New Orleans, Louisiana, January 4-8, 1971 (Nashville, Tennessee: Tidings, 1971).

2. Cf. Bernard Semmel, *The Methodist Revolution* (New York: Basic Books, Inc., 1973).

3. Cf. James Boswell, *Life of Johnson* (3d ed.; 1799), Tuesday, March 31, 1778. Cf. also Wednesday, April 15, 1778, and Tuesday, July 13, 1779.

4. Cf. John Wesley, *A Concise History of England. From the Earliest Times to the Death of George II*. In four volumes (London, 1776 [only the last volume is dated]).

5. Cf. *A Survey of the Wisdom of God in the Creation: or a Compendium of Natural Philosophy*. First edition in two volumes, 1763; second edition in three volumes, 1770; third edition, "enlarged," in *five* volumes, 1777.

6. Cf. "On Christian Doctrine" (*De Doctrina Christiana*), ch. xi, entitled, "Whatever has been rightly said by the heathen, we must appropriate to our own uses."

7. "Moreover, if those who are called philosophers (and especially the Platonists) have said aught that is true and in harmony with our faith, we are not only not to shrink from it but to claim it for our own use." *Idem*, par. 60.

[8] In his diaries, letters, *Journal*, etc.

[9] *Ad populum*, as he says quaintly, in the preface to *Sermons on Several Occasions* (London, 1746).

[10] Cf., e.g.,
Post ignem aethereá domo
Subductum, macies et nova febrium
Terris incubuit cohors; . . .
from *Odes*, Book I, iii. Ins. 29-31. In his sermon on "God's Approbation of His Works," II. 1, in *The Works of John Wesley*, edited by Thomas Jackson (London 1729-31),Vl, pp. 213-14 (hereafter cited as *Works*), Wesley paraphrases these lines, ". . . in plain English, after man, in utter defiance of his Maker, had eaten of the tree of knowledge . . . a whole army of evils, totally new, totally unknown till then, broke in upon rebel man, and all other creatures, and overspread the face of the earth." In his sermon "The Heavenly Treasure in Earthen Vessels," II. 1 (*Works*,VII p. 346), he gives another version, "After man had stolen fire from heaven (what an emblem of forbidden knowledge!) that unknown army of consumptions, fevers, sickness, pain of every kind, fixed their camp upon earth. . . ."
See also, *Si possis, recte; si non, quocunque modo rem* from Horace's *Epistles*, I. 1. 66. In the sermon "On the Education of Children," par. 19 (*Works*,VII, p. 95), Wesley translates, "Get money, honestly if you can; but if not, get money." In "National Sins and Miseries," II. 2 (*Works*,VII, p. 405), he translates, "If you can get money honestly, do; but however, get money." Cf. also the sermon on "The Danger of Riches," par. 1 (*Works*; VII; p. 1) where, without Horace's Latin, Wesley says, "They that will be rich, that is, will be rich at all events, will be rich, right or wrong."

[11] Cf., e.g., *The Aeneid*, Book VI Ins. 726-27: "*Totam,/Mens agitans molem, et magno se corpore miscens,* . . ." ("The all-informing soul, that fills, pervades, and actuates the whole"), which Wesley quotes in his sermons "Of the Church," par. 13 (*Works*, VI, p. 395); "Spiritual Worship," I.5 (*Works*, VI, p. 427), and "On the Omnipresence of God," II. 1 (*Works*,VII, p. 240). See also his *The Doctrine of Original Sin, According to Scripture, Reason and Experience*, Part I, par. I. 13 (*Works*, IX, p. 203).

[12] Aristophanes, Hadrian, Homer, Lucanus, Lucretius, Persius, Pindar, Seneca, Sophocles, Suetonius, Terence, Velleius, Paterculus.

[13] In his letter to the Mayor of Newcastle-upon-Tyne, October 26, 1745, *The Letters of John Wesley*, edited by John Telford (London: Epworth Press, 1931), II, p. 52 (hereafter cited as *Letters*). See also *The Journal of John Wesley*, edited by Nehemiah Curnock (London: Robert Cully, 1909-1916), III, p. 217 (hereafter cited as *Journal*).

[14] Cf. his *Primitive Physick* in its twenty-three editions between 1747 and 1791; remember also his pioneer use of "electrification" as a therapeutic procedure.

[15] Thomas Otway (1652-1685), student of Christ Church before Wesley, wrote two very popular tragedies (*The Orphan* and *Venice Preserv'd* [1682]). Oliver Goldsmith thought Otway was, "next to Shakespeare, the greatest genius England has ever produced in tragedy." Earlier, Richard Steele, in *The Conscious Lovers*, Act II, Sc. 2, had also ranked Otway with Shakespeare.

[16] Curator, Methodist Historical Collection, Bridwell Library.

[17] *Letters*, IV, p. 299. On February 5, 1756, in a letter to William Dodd (*Letters*, III, p. 156), Wesley had written that he "began to make the Scriptures my study (about seven and twenty years ago)."

[18] This phrase has a curious history. Wesley got it in this form from Jeremy Taylor, *Life of Christ*, Part ii., Section 12, Discourse XII, par. 16 in *The Works of Jeremy Taylor*, I, p. 230, but its more common usage was quite opposite: *Cavete hominem unius libri* ("beware of a man of just one book")—i.e., anybody who relies inordinately on a single authority. Archbishop John Tillotson, in his sermon on Luke 16:8, "Wiser Than the Children of Light," says, "It is a saying, I think of Thomas Aquinas, *Cave ab illo gui unicum legit librum*: 'He is a dangerous man that reads but one book' " (*Sermons* [1722], I, p. 565). Despite the legend that this monition goes back to St. Thomas Aquinas, it appears in none of his published writings. More probably, its source was Roger Bacon's complaint against the servile citations of Peter Lombard's *Sentences* as a sufficient authority in settling

disputed theological questions. Cf. Bacon, *Opus minus in Opera quaedam hactenus inedita*, I, pp. 328-29 (1859).

[19] Cf. *Journal*, I, p. 447 (Tuesday, March 23, 1738): "I began the Greek Testament again, resolving to abide by 'the law and the testimony'; and being confident that God would hereby show me whether this doctrine was of God." See also *Letters*, III, p. 332, for his letter to William Law, January 6, 1756: "In every point I appeal 'to the law and the testimony,' and value no authority but this." In his sermon on "The Nature of Enthusiasm," par. 22 (*Works*, V, pp. 473-74), Wesley says we should seek to know and do "the will of God" not by "*particular impressions*" but by appeal "to the law and the testimony."

[20] Cf., e.g., *Journal*, III, p. 17; Wesley's sermon on the "Sermon on the Mount, XII," III. 9 (*Works*, V, p. 421); and "Catholic Spirit," III. 2 (*Works*, V, p. 502).

[21] "Original Sin," par. 4 (*Works*, VI, p. 55).

[22] Cf., e.g., *Journal*, III, p. 17; Wesley's sermon on the "Sermon on the Mount, XII," III. 9 (*Works*, V, p. 421); and "Catholic Spirit," III. 2 (*Works*, V, p. 502).

[23] Cf. Albert C. Outler (ed.), *John Wesley* in *A Library of Protestant Thought* (New York: Oxford University Press, 1964), pp. 146-47 (hereafter cited as LPT *Wesley*): "Q. 14. What books may an Assistant read? A. Sallust, Caesar, Tully, Erasmus, Castellio, Terence, Virgil, Horace, Vida, Buchanan, G. Test., Epictetus, Plato, Ignatius, Ephraim Syrus, Homer, *Greek Epigrams*, Duport, Bp. Ussher's *Sermons*, Arndt, Boehm, Nalson, Pascal, Francke, R. Gell, *our Tracts*." See also *Minutes of Several Conversations* (*Works*, VIII, p. 315) where Wesley admonishes reluctant students, "Contract a taste for reading by use or return to your trade."

[24] Cf. *Works*, X, pp. 480-500.

II: Diagnosing the Human Flaw

1 Cf. his letter to George Downing, April 6, 1761 (*Letters*, IV, p. 146) and his letter to "Various Clergymen," April 19, 1764) (*Letters*, IV, p. 237).

2 Cf. Article VII, "Of Original or Birth Sin," in *The Book of Discipline of The United Methodist Church, 1972*, par. 69, p. 55, where Wesley's abridgment of Article IX of the "Thirty-Nine Articles" of the *Book of Common Prayer* reads as follows: "Original sin standeth not in the following of Adam (as the Pelagians do vainly talk), but in the corruption of the nature of every man, that naturally is engendered of the offspring of Adam, whereby man is very far gone from original righteousness, and of his own nature inclined to evil, and that continually."

See also the former Evangelical United Brethren "Confession," Article VII, "Sin and Free Will," ibid., pp. 62-63: "We believe man is fallen from righteousness and, apart from the grace of our Lord Jesus Christ, is destitute of holiness and inclined to evil. Except a man be born again, he cannot see the Kingdom of God. In his own strength, without divine grace, man cannot do good works pleasing and acceptable to God. We believe, however, man influenced and empowered by the Holy Spirit is responsible in freedom to exercise his will for good."

3 The so-called "Five Points of Calvinism" were easily remembered by their acronym:

1. Total Depravity
2. U-nconditional Election
3. L-imited Atonement
4. I-rresistible Grace
5. P-erseverance of the Saints

4 For the details, cf. the important account of this controversy, from an "evangelical" perspective, in C. F. Allison, *The Rise of Moralism: The Proclamation of the Gospel from Hooker to Baxter* (New York: Seabury Press, 1966).

5 Philip Schaff, *Creeds of Christendom* (New York: Harper & Brothers,

1882), III, pp. 523-24. For the account of this affair that Wesley himself knew best, see Jeremy Collier, *An Ecclesiastical History of Great Britain* (London, 1714), II, pp. 644-45.

[6] Romans 7:21-23.

[7] For example, cf. "Remarks on Mr. Hill's Review" (*Works*, X, p. 403): ". . . I did not see clearly that we are saved by faith till the year 1738. . . ." Also his letter to William Law (*Letters*, I, pp. 239-42), dated May 14, 1738, where Wesley sharply criticizes his old mentor for not having "advised" him of "this living, justifying faith in the blood of Jesus." In his "Farther Appeal . . ." (*Works*, VIII, p. 111), Wesley says he was ordained deacon in 1725 and "during all that time I was utterly ignorant of justification and confounded by sanctification. . . ." In one of his last sermons, "On the Wedding Garment," par. 18 (*Works*, VII, p.317), he says, "Only about fifty years ago [i.e., 1738-40] I had a clearer view than before of justification by faith—and in this time, from that very hour, I never varied. . . ."

[8] Summarized, from the *sola fide side*, in Allison, *Rise of Moralism*, chs. 1,3,4,8.

[9] Job 3:17, "There the Wicked," October 1, 1725;
Matthew 6:33, "Seek Ye First," November 21, 1725;
Psalm 91:11, "On Guardian Angels," September 29, 1726;
2 Samuel 12:23, "On Mourning for the Dead," January 11, 1727;
2 Corinthians 2:17, "On Corrupting the Word of God," October 6,1727;
John 1:47, "On Dissimulation," January 17, 1728;
Exodus 20:8, "On the Sabbath," July 4, 1730;
John 13:7, "What I Do, Thou Canst Not Know," October 13, 1730;
Genesis 1:27, "The Image of God," November 1, 1730;
Proverbs 11:30, "He That Winneth Souls is Wise," July 12, 1731;
Amos 3:6, "Public Diversions," n.d. (probably ca. 1732);
Mark 12:30, "Love of God and Neighbour," September 15, 1733;
Luke 16:8, "Wiser Than the Children of Light," n.d.;
Matthew 6:22, 23, "A Single Intention," February 3, 1736;
1 Corinthians 13:3, "On Love," February 20, 1736;
Isaiah 1:21, "Hypocrisy in Oxford" (English text), June 24, 1741;
(Latin text), June 27, 1741.

[10] *Pugna Spiritualis* (1599); cf. Lawrence Scupoli, *The Spiritual Combat and a Treatise on Peace of the Soul* (Philadelphia: The Westminster Press, 1945).

[11] Edited by Winthrop S. Hudson (Philadelphia: The Westminster Press, 1948).

[12] *Journal*, I, pp. 418-20.

[13] Ibid., pp. 458-59.

[14] Ibid., pp. 475-77.

[15] Ibid., II, pp. 3-63.

[16] Ibid., pp. 83-84.

[17] "In the following week I began more narrowly to inquire what the doctrine of the Church of England is concerning the much-controverted point of justification by faith; and the sum of what I found in the Homilies I extracted and printed for the use of others." Ibid., p. 101.

[18] Ibid., p. 125.

[19] In his letter to John Newton, May 14, 1765 (*Letters*, IV, p. 298).

[20] Wesley's doctrine of Christian perfection is an amalgam of many sources, but its fountainhead (outside the New Testament, of course) is Gregory of Nyssa; cf. LPT *Wesley*, pp. 9-10, note 26.

[21] Cf. Peter Heylyn, *Historia Quinquarticularis* (1659), and Collier, *Ecclesiastical History*.

[22] W. E. H. Lecky, *A History of England in the Eighteenth Century*, New Edition (London: Longmans, Green, and Co., 1892), III, p. 122.

[23] Cf. the doctrinal guidelines specified in the new "Doctrinal Statement," included in *The Discipline of The United Methodist Church*, 1972, Part II, par. 70, pp. 75ff.

[24] "Original Sin," III.5 (*Works*, VI, p. 64).

[25] *The Principles of a Methodist Farther Explained* (*Works*, VIII, pp. 472-73).

[26] Cf. Wesley's sermon "On Wandering Thoughts" (1760+). This sermon did not appear in the first edition of Vol. III of *Sermons on Several Occasions* (1750). It *did* appear, however, in the second edition, inserted between "Christian Perfection" and "Satan's Devices" as No. XII in Vol. III—and in the series that is numbered XXXVI. This second edition bears no date. See E. H. Sugden, *The Standard Sermons of John Wesley* (London: Epworth Press, 1956), II, pp. 178-90.

[27] "On Sin in Believers" (March 28, 1763), No. XLVI, ibid., pp. 360-78.

[28] Cf. "The Scripture Way of Salvation," III.6, ibid., p. 454. See also, "The Deceitfulness of the Human Heart," II.5 (*Works*, VII, 341): ". . . the heart, even of a believer, is not wholly purified when he is justified. Sin is then overcome but it is not rooted out; it is conquered, but not destroyed."

[29] Cf. "Large Minutes" (1744), p. 2: "If a believer wilfully sins, he casts away his faith . . . for a man may forfeit the free gift of God, either by sins of omission or commission."

[30] Cf. Exodus 13:3, 14; 20:2; Deuteronomy 5:6; 6:12; 8:14; 13:5, 10; Joshua 24:17; Judges 6:8.

[31] Romans 8:15.

[32] 2 Thessalonians 2:7.

[33] 1 Timothy 3:16.

III: On "Offering Christ"

[1] Chapter 1, p. 13.

[2] *Journal*, II, p. 243.

[3] Cf. the "Large Minutes" (1744), I, p. 23: "Q. 13. What is the best general method in preaching? A. (1) To invite; (2) to convince; (3) to offer Christ; (4) to build up—and to do this, in some measure, in every sermon."

[4] *Journal*, I, p. 476.

[5] Paul Tillich, *The Shaking of the Foundations* (New York: Charles Scribner's Sons, 1948), p. 162. Cf. Alan Walker, *Jesus the Liberator* (Nashville: Abingdon Press, 1973), p. 47.

[6] Cf. Peter Gay, *The Weimar Culture* (New York: Harper & Row, 1968), for a brilliant account of the culture in which Tillich grew into maturity; see also Hannah Tillich, *From Time to Time* (New York: Stein and Day, 1973), for a libelous account of how Professor Tillich responded to the stimuli of his "liberation."

[7] *Journal*, II, p. 467.

[8] This turning point may be seen in his sermon, "The Lord Our Righteousness" (1765), No. XLIX, Sugden, *Standard Sermons*, II, pp. 420-41.

[9] Cf. *Cur Deus Homo* (1097).

[10] Cf. Romans 1:17; 3:5, 21-26, 30; 5:1; 6:7, etc.

[11] Cf. No. V, Sugden, *Standard Sermons*, I, pp. 112-30.

[12] Cf. No I, ibid., II, pp. 442-60.

[13] Ibid., I, p. 120.

[14] Ibid., pp. 120-21.

[15] Richard Niebuhr, *The Kingdom of God in America* (Chicago: Willett, Clark and Company, 1937), p. 193.

[16] Cf. 1 Corinthians 1:24-30, which, as we saw, was Wesley's favorite text for 1739.

[17] John 3:2. Wesley records that he preached on this text (and context) eighteen times altogether.

IV: "Holiness of Heart and Life"

[1] In *The Book of Discipline*, 1972, par. 334.

[2] The primary texts may be seen in "The Large Minutes" (1766), chiefly from the Leeds Conference of 1766, but with bits and pieces from the first Conference (at the Foundry, 1744), and from "The Twelve Rules of a Helper" (1763). Cf. *Works*, VIII, pp. 309-10.

[3] Wesley's text: "Do you expect to be perfected in love in this life?" ("The Large Minutes," 1766, p. 54).

[4] Wesley's text: "Are you groaning after it?"

[5] See above, p. 23; also chapter 2, note 1.

[6] Cf. "Minutes of Several Conversations Between the Rev. Mr. Wesley and Others From the Year 1744 to the Year 1789," *Works*, VIII, p. 299.

[7] Cf. Wesley's recollection of this conversion, its substance and consequences in *A Plain Account of Christian Perfection*, pars. 2-6 (1766).

[8] See above, p. 31.

[9] Cf. LPT *Wesley*, p. 31. Also, see above, chapter 2, note 19.

[10] Notice his affirmative retrospect of it in *A Plain Account of Christian Perfection*, par. 6, where he says (in 1766) that he had continued in this view of "holy living," "without any material addition or diminution."

[11] Cf. Josiah Tucker, *A Brief History of the Principles of Methodism* (Oxford, 1742).

[12] In Wesley's view, the formal cause of our justification is God's mercy; cf. his pamphlet, *Thoughts on the Imputed Righteousness of Christ* (1762), in *Works*, X, pp. 312-15.

[13] "On God's Vineyard," I.5 (*Works*, VII, p. 204); cf. notes on this passage (including the reference to Castaniza) in LPT *Wesley*, pp. 107-8.

[14] This goes back to Melanchthon's famous *causa concurrens*, and to Bucer's *iustitia duplex* (both of them indebted to Erasmus). It was one of the Bucer-Gropper formulae in *The Book of Ratisbon* (1545); it was advocated by Pole and Seripando at Trent, and also by Bellarmine in the *De Auxillis* controversy. It was one of Cranmer's points in the Homilies which Wesley abridged in his *Doctrine of Salvation, Faith and Good Works* (1738). In short, this is the "catholic" obverse to the "protestant" *sola fide*.

[15] "On God's Vineyard," I.8, 9 (*Works*, VII, pp. 205-6).

[16] Hubert Jedin, "The Opening of the Debate on Justification," in *A History of the Council of Trent* (London: Thomas Nelson, 1961), Vol. II, ch. v, pp. 166-96, and especially the draft decree on justification produced by Girolamo Seripando, pp. 239ff.

[17] Cf. Robert Bellarmine's discussion of the "causes of the justification of the impious" in his *De justificatione*, I, ii., in *De Controversiis Christianae Adversus Huius Temporis Haereticas* (Ingolstadt, 1601), IV, p. 935—especially his comments on "meritorious cause."

[18] Cf. Allison, *Rise of Moralism*, chs. 1, 3, 5, 7, 8.

[19] It may be read in *Works*, VI, pp. 506-13.

[20] Cf. LPT *Wesley*, pp. 298-305.

[21] Cf. the Sermon "On Schism," in *Works*, VI, pp. 401-10.

[22] Cf. Galatians 5:22.

23 Cf. his sermon under this title in LPT *Wesley*, pp. 91–102.

24 Cf. Richard Lucas, *Enquiry After Happiness* (London, 1717), which Wesley read while at Oxford (1730 and following) with evident appreciation. See V.H.H. Green, *The Young Mr. Wesley* (London: Edward Arnold, 1961), pp. 131, 132, 155, 196.

25 As he says in "The Righteousness of Faith," II.9, Sugden, *Standard Sermons*, I, p. 143.

26 "The Important Question," III.2 (*Works*, VI, p. 498).

27 Martin Schmidt has recognized this without quite approving it. Cf. his *John Wesley: A Theological Biography* (Nashville: Abingdon, 1973), II[2], p. 214: "'holiness and happiness' was a formula which had seized and activated him from his youth up." On the following page (215), Schmidt repeats himself: "'Holiness and happiness' is [Wesley's] favorite formula."

28 Cf. "The Original, Nature, Property, and Use of the Law," "The Law Established Through Faith, I," and "The Law Established Through Faith, II," in Sugden, *Standard Sermons*, II, pp. 37–83.